MEMORIES

Yorkshire Fishing Industry

Ron Freethy

COUNTRYSIDE BOOKS
NEWBURY BERKSHIRE

COUNTRYSIDE BOOKS
3 Catherine Road
Newbury, Berkshire

To view our complete range of books,
please visit us at
www.countrysidebooks.co.uk

ISBN 978 1 84674 264 4

Designed by Peter Davies, Nautilus Design

Produced through MRM Associates Ltd., Reading
Typeset by Jean Cussons Typesetting, Diss, Norfolk
Printed by Berforts Information Press, Oxford

Contents

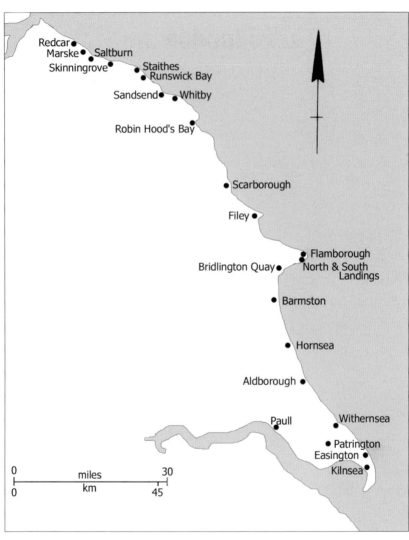

Map of the fishing stations operating on the Yorkshire coast in the late 18th and early 19th centuries.

Introduction and Acknowledgements

Hull, in its heyday, was the largest and most important fishing port in Britain, quite apart from its commercial docks and all their associated trades. Statistics place it ahead of both Grimsby in old Lincolnshire on the opposite side of the Humber and the Lancashire trawling port of Fleetwood. It must not be assumed, however, that until the growth of Hull, fishing along the Yorkshire coast was unimportant – indeed, it was vital. There were important fleets at Bridlington, Filey, Scarborough and Whitby, as well as at the villages of Flamborough, Robin Hood's Bay, Runswick and Staithes. This book tells their story, from the far-off days of whaling at Whitby and trawling at Hull to the sad decline that has seen so many seamen seek other employment and once-bustling docks redeveloped into leisure facilities. Our inshore fishing fleets do still survive, though, at the smaller ports along the coast. Most of them are now classed as seaside resorts and the casual visitor often does not realise just what a rich and fascinating history they have.

The secret of enjoying the history of the Yorkshire fishing industry involves two aspects. Visits to the museums described in later chapters are vital and the chance should be taken to talk to the volunteers who help to staff these places. They will often have salt water history flowing through their veins and are only too willing to talk so don't feel embarrassed by showing interest. Secondly, go down to the harbour and buy fish or take a pleasure trip and talk fishing to the boatmen – you will not be disappointed.

As a result of the Millennium celebrations of the year 2000, I was asked by the BBC to write and present four one-hour radio documentaries on the history of the seaside resorts of Yorkshire. I began by writing to the Tourist Department and was put in touch with Kevin Barrand, who had done a considerable amount of research on the subject. He provided me with a list of contacts, including curators, hoteliers and, in the context of this book, with the fishermen of Whitby, Scarborough, Filey and Bridlington, as well as those who still fish in and around the villages of the area. I have tapes of these interviews and have kept in touch with some of those who were interviewed during the programmes and their memories have been invaluable to me.

I am also lucky in having lots of friends and family associated with the trawling industry in Fleetwood, Grimsby and Hull. Although there has always been rivalry between the three major trawling ports of Britain, they are all united as they face a common enemy – the sea.

Many of the men and women to whom I have spoken are mentioned in the relevant chapters and, apart from recording their invaluable contributions, I need do little more. There are, however, a number of people, including Kevin Barrand, who warrant a very special word of thanks. They are Mr and Mrs Harry Chantler, Dick Gillingham, Mick Rodgers, Lionel Marr and Derek Keetley.

I must give special mention to the books written by Alec Gill who has made a wonderful job of recording the lives of fisherfolk all around Hull. His photographic records in and around the Hessle Road area are a unique record of a proud yet bygone age.

With any book recording memories of those who lived and worked during the heyday of a particular industry, artefacts and photographs always have an invaluable impact. The fact that I have been able to locate so many images has been largely due to the researching abilities of Keith Hall and whilst he explained his finds to me, his wife Mary kept us all well supplied with tea and cakes.

I must again give credit to my publishers whose editorial and planning skills are always a source of pleasure for me. Finally, for a man who feels at ease writing with an ancient fountain pen, I give special thanks to my wife for her patience, clear thinking and word processing skills. Marlene, as always, is the workhorse of our long partnership.

Ron Freethy

Chapter 1

The Origins of Yorkshire Fishing

These days it is often said that there is no major port between Hull on the Humber and Sunderland on the Wear, and then on to Newcastle-upon-Tyne, but the old Yorkshire ports of Staithes, Runswick, Robin Hood's Bay, Flamborough, Bridlington, Filey, Scarborough and Whitby are still in operation and of great interest to the historian and those in search of memories of the good old days of the fishing industry.

Not only were there large fleets of commercial fishing vessels along the Yorkshire coastline, but each village and inlet made part of its living from the harvest of the sea. This was even the case at Flamborough Head, which is made up of some of the highest chalk cliffs to be found anywhere along the coast of Britain. The seas around the Head are treacherous and the lighthouses built on the headland have long been vital to fishermen and merchant seamen who rely on these structures to warn them of rocks.

Aerial view of Flamborough Head in the 1950s.

The so-called New Lighthouse is actually not so new, having been completed in 1806 and is now the focus for an extensive car park with an associated crop of gift shops and cafés. Many visitors driving towards the 'new' tower overlook the even older lighthouse built from chalk in 1674 and therefore one of the oldest such structures still standing in Britain. Some historians, using more sentimentality than fact, have suggested that the name Flamborough derives from 'the flame of fire' which burned on top of the old lighthouse. The name is much older than this, however, and almost certainly derives from the Saxon word *flaen* which means 'arrow head'. This is certainly the shape of Flamborough Head when viewed from the sea.

Flamborough had two landing areas. At the North Landing a lifeboat station was established in 1871. Here, and also at South Landing, fishermen traditionally based their vessels but landing was never easy and the cobles (flat-bottomed, open fishing boats, with high bows) had to be hauled up to the safety of the beach. Way back in the 1950s I met Billy Dove, who later became a schoolmaster and who described to me the fishing traditions of his native village. Billy told me that even by 1902, visitors from as far away as Leeds would delight the local folk by arriving to see the fishing landings and the lighthouse.

One of the sights of the North Landing used to be the fish auctions which were traditionally held on the sands. Donkeys were lined up with wicker baskets strapped to their flanks and the catch was carried up onto the cliff tops and away to markets in the local villages. In the days when refrigeration was still far into the future, all fish and seafood had to be sold and eaten quickly.

Bridlington has often been dismissed as merely a 19th-century, sea-bathing town of spa proportions but it was once the major port of the old East Riding of Yorkshire. It could be argued too, that in terms of tracing the history of the Yorkshire fishing industry, Filey is an ideal starting point. Although it evolved

The 1806 Flamborough lighthouse.

into a rather refined seaside resort, it developed from a cluster of fishermen's cottages and many of these remain standing to this day. In season, fishing and tourist trips operate from the harbour and many who take advantage of the tours do not realise that they are sailing in a piece of wonderful history. Both Scarborough and Whitby further up the coast were fishing villages first, and

In the early days of lifeboats, several men and horses were required to launch the boats, as seen here at Filey.

THE HARBOUR, BRIDLINGTON.

Bridlington harbour in the mid 20th century.

only later developed into tourist hotbeds. Whitby is actually even more historic than the other resorts. It is an ancient whaling and fishing port, as well as a centre of religion, with its magnificent Benedictine abbey dominating the headland that overlooks the harbour.

Close to Whitby is the hamlet of Raw, thought to be the point at which the first settlement, now known as Robin Hood's Bay, was established. The people here survived by a combination of fishing and farming but eventually chose to live further up from the harbour because of the constant harassment by pirates. Fishing in the village continued for centuries. During the 19th century, Robin Hood's Bay was the most important fishing base along the coast, with more than 150 men working out of the harbour. At that time there were more boats operating here than at either Whitby or Scarborough. The fishwives walked miles along what

Robin Hood's Bay, 1950.

were called pannier ways (basket roads) and tracks leading to inland markets. These days only a very few fishermen are based around the village.

This is a treacherous coast and, for a while, Robin Hood's Bay ran its own lifeboat service until a Royal National Lifeboat Station was set up in 1881. More than 100 people were plucked safely from the sea prior to the station being disbanded in 1931. Obviously the

A view of the town at Robin's Hoods Bay, 1901.

11

recruitment of lifeboat crews was almost totally dependent upon the enthusiasm and bravery of the fishermen. One of the most celebrated rescues was in 1881 when conditions were so extreme that a more modern boat from Whitby had to be dragged overland to the bay by horses. Four miles off the coast was a 209-ton ship called the *Visitor* struggling in stormy seas. It took two attempts to get the lifeboat out but the crew were eventually successful and the six men aboard the stricken vessel were brought back safe and sound.

In some cases, ships were caught on the rocks close to cliffs overlooking Robin Hood's Bay. This led to the construction of what has been known as Rocket Post Field. Here was a post which was used to practise cliff rescues. A rocket with a very long rope attached was fired from the post towards the stranded ship and along this lifeline the crew could climb to safety. It is thought that this was the origin of the breeches buoy system which is used to this day to transfer stranded mariners from one ship to another.

There was a ribbon of fishing villages between Whitby and Hull. Between 1789 and 1825 there was no substantial fishing fleet at Whitby because this port concentrated very heavily on whaling, but at that time there were 36 fleets operating between Staithes and Flamborough. Nine of these were based at Staithes; by 1825 there were 39 fleets with 17 sailing out of Staithes. These boats were fitted out each March and had a crew of up to five. At the end of the summer they joined in with a substantial herring fleet and made their way southwards along the

A Yorkshire lugger – this vessel had a five-man crew and many of these boats operated out of Staithes.

coast. They did this because they followed the migration of the fish which at one time made up an important part of the diet, especially for the poor. These five-man crews operated in what were known as Yorkshire luggers. They invariably worked under contract to companies mainly based in Great Yarmouth. My Uncle Albert hailed from Great Yarmouth and his father and grandfather made their living from the herring fisheries. The crews were paid 'steerage money' to cover their basic costs and then were paid on the weight of fish they brought into the ports.

Drift nets were important for the catching of herring; the net is hung just beneath the surface and to the lay person looks a bit like a huge net curtain supported by floats. Herring shoals come to the surface at night and the fish trap their gills in the mesh which they cannot see in the dark. A drifter can carry as many as 70 net sections, each measuring up to 150 ft in length. Unlike trawlers, a drifter brings its catch fresh to port each day.

The herring fleet differed from all the others by moving from one port to another to deliver the catch close to the southerly migratory movement of the herring. I began to understand this when I worked with Tony Dalton, who in the 1980s operated a couple of converted trawlers to provide Natural History tours of the Outer Hebrides; I was the resident naturalist on these tours. These vessels, the *Pentland Wave* and the *St Just*, plied their trade out of Mallaig. Whilst I was around this lovely harbour I got to know some ladies with memories of the herring trade which carried on into the 1970s. Jenny Cockburn told me,

My grandma often told me of the Herring Girls who she said were lasses from the English ports who followed the fishing fleets as they pursued the shoals along the coast. They came from places such as Scarborough and Hull in search of adventure. Although they worked hard, many managed to find husbands. The girls were lodged in organised digs ruled over by morally aware landladies. The lasses were given a modest signing-on fee, rail fare and travelling box labels but had to provide their own clothes and sharp knife.

Skipper Tony Dalton (centre left) fishing for pleasure from the Pentland Wave in 1978

The preparation of a herring into a kipper involved four stages, which could roughly be divided into splitting the fish, soaking it in brine, hanging the fish on tenterhooks and smoking it. When the Herring Girls reached Hull there was a designated area where the girls split the fish. They were also paid to strip the flesh off the bones and separate other pieces which were then collected by a nearby fishmeal factory. Jenny Cockburn continued,

These girls worked hard and their language according to my grandma would even shock the men but they had a fantastic sense of humour. They needed it because even on a so-called 'normal' day which was from 6 am to 6 pm there were times when the lasses could not finish until the last of the fish was pushed into the smoke house.

The smoke house was the province of a man who began the process by setting fire to his own favourite mix, but it always involved sawdust. The smoking went on overnight and the fish were then boxed and sent to market. My daughter-in-law is Danish and I have spent some time there watching the traditional way of smoking herrings, as well as producing kippers. This really was a blast from the past and the herring industry at Fåborg must have been the same as in Scarborough and Hull, as the Herring Girls moved to keep up with the fish.

Historians are certain that herring kippering dates back to Viking times and the method has changed very little since. I remember visiting Jack Fortune's smoke house on Henrietta Street in Whitby

Sorting the fish at Scarborough.

Scotch Fisher Girls at Scarborough

and being shown the bags of oak chippings which were used. Jack was adept at stripping herrings on rods ready for smoking. He once told me that kippers were like people he did not trust – 'Two-faced and no guts,' he grinned.

Jenny Cockburn went on,

We have a good collection of old photographs, one of which we think was taken in Bridlington which had my grandmother in it. She followed the herring for more than 30 years. I still love to eat herring, however it is cooked, but neither my mum or gran would touch them. I suppose they had more than enough of them when they were working. It does seem strange that a gradual decline in the demand for herring, in the first half of the 19th century, was not determined by events focused around Britain. Much of the salted herring catch was exported to the West Indies and the Southern States of America where the fish was fed to the slaves. However, from 1835 onwards the idea of using slave labour was frowned upon and few, if any exporters, would trade with the plantation owners. Another market which evaporated even more quickly was in Ireland, as a result of the potato famine of the 1840s. Their people were literally starving and had no money to buy fish, however cheap it may have been. To compensate for this, there was an increased demand in England due to the expansion of the railways, providing ready markets for an increased working population.

At this time the soon-to-be famous fish trains came into being. The Railway Fish Carriage Agreement meant that each of the many railway companies agreed to work together to ensure that fish from the ports reached the inland towns and cities fresh. Fish wagons were attached to goods trains and these were constructed specifically to handle the fish. The last word on the herring trade in this chapter has to come from Margaret Knowles, who remembers those days well,

We lived near to Hull docks and well into the 1980s I remember when a fish train was passing. There would be carriages attached

to 'normal' trains and going to places such as Leeds or Bradford. If there was a breeze in the right direction, the smell of fish was very obvious!

Jack Fortune at his smoke house on Henrietta Street, Whitby.

Chapter 2

Whitby, Staithes and Robin Hood's Bay

Whitby is a wonderful place full of friendly folk around the harbour willing to talk fish and fishing, but with a tradition of whaling which is reflected in the names of the steep narrow streets and the quaint cottages. Here are some of the best fish and chip shops and it is *the* place to sample the finest fresh crab to be found anywhere in Britain. Close to the town centre and with a number of convenient car parks nearby is Whitby Museum, which tells the story of the development of Whitby and is well worth a visit.

I love buying fresh fish and crabs direct from the quay and have even caught my own fish – usually mackerel – during boat trips from the harbour, in between being seasick. I knew that I was a landlubber when the *Rose Marie* dropped her anchor to allow us to fish and the vessel began to rock and roll. Our boatman gave me a knowing smile, took over my line and caught lots of fish for me to take home.

The inner harbour, Whitby, in the mid 20th century.

I was much more comfortable a few years later when I was commissioned by BBC Radio to write and present a history of Whitby. I clambered aboard a fishing boat to interview Gordon Quinn, who told me of the problems faced by modern-day heroes who try to wrest a living from the sea. It is not so much that the sea is cruel but rather that the fishing quotas have begun to bite. Gordon told me,

The vessels we use are under 10 metres – notice I've gone metric – but this means that we can get in close. My main income comes from crabs and lobsters, with our main markets in France and Spain. I'll bet if you have sea food in these countries they will be British in origin. And they say French food is the best! We are lucky at Whitby in that we can get into and out of the harbour at all states of the tide. This means that my working day can be from 5 am to 5 pm.

Crabs and lobsters are at their best from April to August and at this time I can be operating 1,000 pots which have to be checked every day. They are secured to the sea bottom and are marked by buoys.

Each fisherman has his own area and you need to remember that once a pot has revealed a catch it has to be baited again with fish offal. We have to make a living in all weathers so when it gets too rough to lift the pots we drift net for salmon. Here we want a stiff wind off the sea. A good catch of salmon means a good pay day but our licence to fish costs thousands so we need to be efficient at our jobs. In the winter, crabs and lobsters need time to breed – remember we are farmers and have to conserve our stocks. At this time of the year we still have to go out and we catch mainly cod by using gill nets.

WORK AND LEISURE, WHITBY · *F.M.S. 44242*

Tourists exploring Whitby harbour in the 1950s.

I love this life but it is getting harder all the time. Our biggest worry now is the cost of diesel which is going up all the time. People think that my work is done when I have landed my catch. Don't forget that I have to repair nets and the lobster pots. Ask any of the lads on this quay and they will tell you that they have always been fishermen and times will have to get really bloody bad afore we give it up.

Catching fish, lobsters and crabs in all weathers is always back-breaking, physically demanding and often dangerous, as Gordon

Many fishermen's wives earned a living by collecting shellfish such as cockles and periwinkles from the shore as seen here at Whitby, c.1920.

Quinn well knows. There is, however, no point in putting life and limb at risk if the catch cannot be sold – properly packaged and presented in a marketable manner. I discovered how this was achieved in Whitby when I spoke to Doris Kavanah. She told me,

I can trace my family back on my father's side to the long gone days of whaling in the 1780s and this was also the case with my husband's family. I followed my mother in learning how to dress crabs for sale in the town. I did this from the 1950s until I retired in 1987.

Crabs have not been everybody's favourite food and the poet Alfred, Lord Tennyson (1809–1892) visited Whitby and was not at all impressed. He was made very ill by what he described as crab poisoning but he had also consumed a full bottle of vintage port which can't have done him a lot of good.

There are still some shops in the side streets of Whitby which sell fish, shellfish and especially dressed crabs. Doris Kavanah also pointed me in the right direction to discover the history of whaling in Whitby and I found that there are tangible reminders of this time. I began by strolling around the town between the harbour and the abbey, which is reached by a lung-bursting climb mounting flight after flight of steps – the total number of steps has been counted at 199. I looked for the names of cottages and little cul-de-sacs. Here I found Harpooners Cottage and an area called Arguments Yard, which some say was an area where payments were negotiated by tough whaling men.

An early 20th-century postcard showing the view towards East Cliff, Whitby, on which stands the parish church and the abbey.

It was near this yard that I met Harry Collet, who was one of the informative tour guides operating around the town. A detailed account of whalers and whaling is given in Chapter 7, but Harry provided me with a brief history of the whaling industry in Whitby,

You can tell that Whitby was a true whaling port by the fact that a prominent headland is dominated by the huge jawbone of a whale, which is in the form of an archway. You should not talk about Whitby's whaling without reference to two Williams – a father and son called Scoresby. It was William senior who invented the 'crow's nest' at the top of a vessel, which was originally designed for a member of crew to keep a look out for whales. His son William junior, born in 1789, was the most famous of the two and he had two strings to his bow. Like his father he became a tough and very successful whaling captain and his ship called Resolution *was famous for its successful catches. He was also very literate and observant and wrote up his Arctic Journals. These were published and resulted in William Scoresby being elected as a Fellow of the Royal Society. Like his father before him, William junior was a skilled inventor and refined the design of a compass which was so impressive that it was adopted by the Admiralty. He later took Holy Orders and became a much loved vicar of Bradford.*

21

I went on to ask Harry what life was like aboard a whaler and his answer surprised me,

> *First, Ron, let me begin with an argument. Most people do not understand the origins of Argument Yard. Actually, Thomas Argument owned a cottage on the headland and as the town grew he sold his garden and the purchaser built houses on the site. This was more of an agreement than an argument. What were once gardens have now become squares of houses. The alleyways leading to these we call snickets or gorts. If you want to understand the development of Whitby as a whaling and fishing port, you must visit the parish church of St Mary dating to the 12th century and situated on the hill overlooking the quay, close to the Abbey.*

It was here that I met Margaret Grundy, who was the Maid of the Church. She explained her role and also proved to be a fount of knowledge in terms of the whaling, fishing and boat building history of the town,

> *My title of Maid is, I think, unique but all I am is a female verger and my function is to control the running of the church. We have never had a verger and there has been an illustrious list of Maids of Whitby Church. Whitby has always earned its living, like the rest of coastal Yorkshire, from a combination of farming and fishing. At first the congregation was small but as the whaling and fishing industries developed there were more and more worshippers and the church was extended. Money was provided by local gentry and ship owners and the labour provided by craftsmen who were almost always shipbuilders. This explains the fact that the interior of our church looks very like a ship.*
>
> *Whaling was a very smelly trade and the ships could be identified by the stench which surrounded them. With so many whalers tied up on the quay and with the wind in the right – or should I say, the wrong – direction, Whitby literally smelt of money. Between 1753 and 1833, 1,761 whales were killed by Whitby ships and supplied*

Whalebone scrapers hard at work – this illustration is from Walker's Costume of Yorkshire, *published in 1814.*

the essential oil for lighting the lamps of Britain – and the bones were much sought after by the makers of ladies' corsets.

Whilst researching this book I also came into contact with Simon Heyhoe, who was then the curator of Fleetwood Museum. Simon recalled the museum holding an exhibition on the history of corsets, which concentrated on the production of whalebone and how this was used to squeeze ladies' bodies into shape: 'It must have been very painful for ladies who did not conform to the standard shape!'

'Boom and bust' is not just a modern concept, it also applied to the whaling industry. Money was easy to generate in the late 18th century but, by 1837, demand had drained away and the last Whitby vessel arrived home empty. Margaret Grundy takes up the history of Whitby whaling,

Some have suggested that this demise was due to over fishing but this was not the only reason. Coal gas had been discovered and whale oil was no longer in demand. Fashions were also changing. There is no doubt that the whale men felt the squeeze but by this time more and more mariners were finding alternative berths in the developing fishing vessels. This town has always been and still is resilient. I was born in the town and can see how vibrant it is.

This is certainly true and, apart from the Scoresby family, Whitby has connections with one of the most famous mariners the world has ever seen. Captain James Cook (1728–1779) well deserves his reputation, as I discovered when I visited the museum dedicated to his life and spoke to its curator, Andrew Milton,

I know you are interested mainly in the history of the fishing industry and we have lots of information concerning this aspect of Whitby's history. All the ships made famous by Cook during his epic South Seas explorations were built in Whitby and the Adventure, Resolution *and especially the* Endeavour *were built at the Fishburn shipyard. These vessels were flat bottomed, which may have made them wobble a bit in heavy weather but it meant they were able to land in very shallow bays. Vessels of this type were also ideal for carrying coal and for fishing in shallow waters. Cook was apprenticed to the Quaker ship owner James Walker, and the museum has been based around this period. I know I'm biased but nobody interested in ship design with regard to fishing, whaling and merchant ships in general should ever miss the chance to come and talk to us.*

During our conversation, Andrew Milton told me that if I wanted to understand Whitby's fishing history I should stand in Town Square and soak up the atmosphere. This is the area of the Old Fish Pier which is now dominated by the RNLI Lifeboat Station. One of the buildings hereabouts was the Burberry raincoat factory. In recent years it has been the ambition of country folk wishing to strike a pose to wear a Burberry but it was much more functional in the old days and was obviously a must for whalers and sailors. Look up to see a golden weather vane in the form of a fish – highly appropriate!

In the first chapter, Robin Hood's Bay was briefly mentioned and although it has long been dominated by Whitby, this was not always the case. In medieval times, according to the monastic records from Whitby Abbey, Robin Hood's Bay had more vessels and enjoyed larger catches than either Whitby or Scarborough.

What present-day Health and Safety officers would make of this fish market in the early 20th century doesn't bear thinking about!

Fisherwives would often tour the town offering fish for sale on cottage doorsteps.

Herring girls at Whitby harbour displaying the catch.

There has, however, never been what you would call a true harbour or even a safe landing in very rough weather and this must have been a constant worry for all fishermen and their families. There were plenty of fish in the near waters, though, and there were also plentiful supplies of both crabs and lobsters. At the end of the day

25

Fisherfolk at work in Whitby, late 19th century.

the cobles had to be hauled up high above the high watermark. Then the catch itself had to be transported up the very steep hill and, from the 1850s onwards, taken to the railway stations and onwards to the lucrative markets of the hungry industrial towns. In the end it was its lack of size which spelt the death knell for the successful commercial fishing from the bay. Many fishermen decided to ply their undoubted skills elsewhere. Some found the Merchant Navy to be the answer but others moved to the larger fishing ports along the Yorkshire coast. Many became mates and skippers but only a very few took a financial gamble and purchased their own vessels.

The impressive lifeboat station at Robin Hood's Bay still stands and, for a time, it was used as a Marine Research Laboratory by Sheffield University. It is now a lifeboat museum, operated during the season by local volunteers. Outside is a large model of a fish with its mouth open and begging for visitors to help to contribute to the running of the museum. Almost opposite are the Bramblewick tearooms and restaurant. The building dates to 1620 and was converted from three fishermen's cottages. On the quayside is the Bay Hotel, much used by the local fisherfolk.

Apart from fishing, the local boatmen had other forms of income: one illegal. All this I discovered when I spoke some years ago to Kevin Barrand, who was then the Tourism Officer for a large stretch of the North Yorkshire coast. As we walked together down the steep steps to the harbour, Kevin told me,

> *Just look how close together the cottages are and how each is perched on a solid shelf of rock. We know that it was possible to walk through one house into another and go from top to bottom of the bay without using the road. It is no wonder that smuggling was rife here in the 18th century and that almost all of those involved avoided capture. Spirits and tobacco arrived in the bay and were soon on their way inland. Another thing you should look out for are buildings with outside doors close to bedroom windows. These were needed because the steps down were so narrow that when somebody died and became stiff they could not be got downstairs and out of the door to be buried. These 'corpse windows' were built specifically for this purpose.*

The Whitby fishermen have always been an adaptable breed and for a time they made a side-line income by taking advantage of the developing industry based around Port Mulgrave. In the 19th century, the Mulgrave Ironstone Company built a harbour in order to export ironstone from their mines. This development cost £45,000 which was a huge financial outlay at this time. The present dilapidated appearance belies the fact that here was once a busy port and one where many a local fisherman could find work on the vessels. Look out for a tunnel near the foot of the cliffs because for nearly a century before it closed in 1920, there was a railway track here, originally operated using horses led inland for nearly a mile and into the stone mines to the south. The ore was carried along the narrow-gauge track and the wagons tipped directly into the holds of the waiting coasters. It was then sent mainly to the iron ore furnaces at Jarrow which was building more and more iron-clad ships. A decline set in from the closure in the 1920s and, at the onset of the Second World War, the facility was destroyed so that it could be of no use to the Germans should the invasion of Britain become a reality.

I asked Kevin if there was still some fishing in the bay and he put me in touch with John Brown, who was both a good fisherman and an accomplished cook. I spoke to him for a long time whilst enjoying his unique brand of fish soup. He told me that it was still possible to make a living by fishing from the bay,

> *There is good fishing here but you do need to be aware of the wind. It's no good trying to fish into an easterly wind because it is asking for trouble. We have a saying in these parts which tells us that 'Wind in the east, fish is least'. By far the best fishing is when a south-west wind is blowing because it enables you to operate closer to the shelter of the cliffs. It always makes me laugh when weather forecasters try to predict our local weather. Fisher folk take no notice – we have always known the best weather for fishing. My boat is only 17 ft long and it allows me to operate in shallow water. In the summer season I mostly catch crabs and lobsters and people ask which of the two is best. I have a saying that the only person who says that crab is better is the person who cannot afford to buy a lobster!*

Robin Hood's Bay was made famous in the middle of the 20th century by the author Leo Walmsley whose novels included *The Lobster Pot* (also called *The Phantom Lobster*); in his books, Robin Hood's Bay became 'Baytown'. I always thought that one lobster pot was the same as any other but John Brown soon put me right,

> *To a fisherman, his pots are his livelihood and they have to be kept in good repair. They are made of supple wood but these days there is a tendency to use metal traps. I don't like this because if you lose one, it doesn't rot away and is a constant killing area. Fishermen should always be conservationists and if we aren't, those*

who follow us will be out of a job. I have another point to make and that is that you can catch crabs anytime but lobsters are more easily potted just before dawn. I am convinced that once it gets light lobsters can escape from even the best-made pots. I'm sure of this although some fishermen don't believe it.

While we were talking, John was busy preparing his fish soup and as he worked away he dispelled a myth. I had often thought that chefs made fish soup from the cheapest possible ingredients. John grinned at me and said,

This is not true if you want to enjoy a full meal of soup. You prepare it in two processes before mixing the two together. I always choose the best fish that I have but with a base of cod. This one I have now has a slice or two of halibut and monkfish and I add a few prawns. I put the fish in a bowl with a dash of lemon juice. I first prepare the base by using a chicken stock. I have tried fish stock but I prefer the chicken. I simmer this and then start adding coriander, paprika, chillies and curry. Gradually I add red peppers, ginger and garlic after frying them in butter. Even this can taste wonderful without adding the fish. Keep tasting and add milk. As this brew simmers, add the fish but do not do much stirring. You want to have lumps of fish and not a paste. I finish off with a pint of cream and serve

Repairing nets on Whitby quay in the early 20th century.

piping hot with lots of crusty bread. This is not a starter but is a full meal and you can vary it depending on your budget.

Before I left him, but with a full stomach, John told me that in the old days fisherfolk would make soup from what they had available at the time and even included crabs' legs, which added to the flavour. I went down to the harbourside where colourful boats were tied up and there were piles of lobster pots and nets in various states of repair. I took time to smell the pots but I did not linger too long. I could smell the bait! John Brown uses the heads of plaice but his rivals have their own favourites.

I moved quickly away from this stench as I wanted to keep the taste of John Brown's fish soup firmly in my memory. During the evening I re-read Leo Walmsley's *The Lobster Pot* and prepared myself for a trip to Scarborough, the subject of the next chapter.

Before I leave Whitby, however, there are two more things which should be described, namely the Whitby jet industry and unusual workers who were needed to support the fishing.

I was given a full account of the history of Whitby jet by Alec McKenzie who told me,

Whitby jet has been used to produce jewellery since the Bronze Age and the Romans exported it all over their empire. There was also a period of great prosperity in the Whitby area in mid-Victorian times when Queen Victoria ordered lots of the black material as she mourned the death of her beloved husband Prince Albert. The jet only occurs in the Whitby area and was produced when a huge forest was inundated by the sea and the wood pressed into a very hard material which was almost stone-like in its consistency. This flooding occurred during the Jurassic period some million years ago. It can be found washed up on the local beaches but also in the nets of fishermen and it is from them that most of my material comes. Some of the men still make a good living from selling bits of jet. I grind and polish this into jewellery. At one time there were many jet workshops operating in Whitby but these days I'm pretty well on my own.

A 1950s' view of Staithes.

Staithes, just to the north of Whitby, was once among the major fishing ports along the north-east coast and produced one of the greatest explorers that the world has ever known – James Cook. There is still some fishing in Staithes and cobles can still be seen lined up along the beach and harbour. The area was constantly raided in the 18th and early 19th centuries by the Navy's press gangs and it is known that many Staithes men were there at the heart of the action with Admiral Lord Nelson at the battle of Trafalgar in 1805. Sandwiched between the headlands of Crowbar Nab and Penny Nab, a maze of cobbled streets lead directly to the harbour. One of the most attractive of these streets is the Dog Loup which is said to be the narrowest in the area and at one point has a width of only 18 inches. Clustered around the harbour are the feeder becks, including Roxby Beck.

It was whilst I was working in Australia during the 1990s that I got to know Anne Hibbert, who told me,

> *My great-grandmother was born and bred in Whitby but I'll bet you will never guess what her job was. She worked as a water-carrier. These days you can go to any harbourside throughout the world and you will find pipes providing fresh water for the ships. This was not the case years ago but ships still needed plentiful supplies of fresh water. Women were employed as water carriers and they made the steep journeys from the springs down to the harbour. Some women took the water in jugs which they carried on their heads. How they kept their balance I don't know, but my great-grandma had a yoke with buckets attached at each end. These days we young folk think we have a tough life but we really do have it easy.*

Anne Hibbert made me aware of a job which would have been part of most English towns and cities but 'water lasses' of the Yorkshire

coast must have been a real tough breed. Now, every time I see old photographs of fishing harbours, I spare more than a passing thought for the water-carriers. All these ports have fascinating histories and I am well aware that I have only scratched the surface. It is now time, however, to move on to Scarborough.

Water-carriers loading up from a spring at Filey.

Chapter 3

Scarborough

Although the Vikings exercised a great influence upon this stretch of the East Coast, and although the Romans occupied many a cliff-top site above the bays, it was the Norsemen who gave Scarborough its name. It means the stronghold of a chieftain named *Skarthi*. The view of the impressive harbour from the solid and splendid Norman castle now managed by English Heritage is so panoramic that this is by far the best place to begin a study of the town. There is plenty of pay-and-display parking at the castle which is open on most days of the year.

Here can be seen an inner harbour still used by cargo and fishing vessels and an outer harbour which is becoming used more and more by private pleasure craft. The history of both harbours is graphically explained within the old lighthouse which has been set up as a museum. The North Bay is the most exposed which accounts for the fact that the harbour is set in the sheltered South Bay. When I spoke to the then Tourism Officer, Kevin Barrand, he told me,

Obviously for you the place to start is at the harbour. You should take your time and stroll around amongst the ropes, chains, crab and lobster pots, fish boxes and, of course, the fishing vessels. You should also look at the computer-controlled lighthouse which actually has a different function to that which you might think.

A 1950s' view of Scarborough's North Bay and harbour.

Scarborough harbour in the late 19th century, with the lighthouse in the background.

Unlike Whitby where boats can enter the harbour whatever the state of the tide, Scarborough does not have this advantage. This problem is solved by the lighthouse. The light flashes whenever the water in the harbour is deep enough to allow vessels to enter. Another thing to remember is to get to the harbour early and speak to the men unloading their catches as it is here that local chefs arrive to select their 'dish of the day'.

I followed Kevin's advice and there I met fisherman Fred Normandale, who was a mine of information with regard to fishing in Scarborough,

The harbour is the focal point of the town in my view and tourists should not be afraid to talk to the fishermen. We don't have all the quayside facilities of larger ports like Hull but we are modern and equipped well enough to do a good job. I have four 60-ft-long trawlers which operate as far afield as Norway, Shetland and the North Sea. They catch mainly cod, whiting and haddock, all of which live close to the seabed, and this is the area operated by our trawls. Usually we auction the catch at the harbourside itself but if we have had a good trip, some fish may be taken to Hull. Our boats operate for 52 weeks in the year except when laid up for repairs and painting. Summer fishing is relatively easy but the North Sea can be a cruel place in winter. You try eating, sleeping and going to the toilet when your whole world is moving. If you want to hear really colourful language, stand close to a cook in his galley during a storm. In good fishing areas the trawl nets may be hauled five times a day and the gear also has to be repaired so you only sleep if you are lucky. Your wages are dependent upon the fish you catch so there is plenty of incentive but in your brief spells at home all you want is to sleep, eat, keep warm and dry and go to the toilet without everything moving about.

It was Fred's grandfather who was the first to operate screw-powered steam trawlers, i.e. trawlers using a propeller system. He was skipper of the *Otter* and devised a system to keep the net open

Laying out the catch on the quay, c.1920s.

during fishing. Two heavy wooden boards were employed and ever since these have been known as 'otterboards'.

It is often assumed that trawling was changed from sail to steam in one leap with the introduction of propellers but there was a step in between. This was the use of paddle steamers. These proved to be a hazard in rough seas and so were soon discontinued. Most of the Yorkshire paddle trawlers were based in Scarborough but many ended their working days as pleasure steamers.

Speaking with Fred Normandale inspired me to spend several early mornings at the fish auctions and then move from the quay to follow the chefs to their local fish and chip shops and restaurants. Firstly my task was to read the menus to see which establishments were offering 'catches of the day'. Over the years I have had long conversations with Harry Chantler, who was a trawler skipper sailing out of Fleetwood who, along with his wife, also enjoyed holidays in Scarborough. Harry gave me some good advice with regard to eating fish,

All fishermen know which species are at their best at which time of the year. When you visit any fishing quay whether it is huge or

Herring girls at work near the outer pier in Scarborough, c.1895.

The herring fleet anchored off Scarborough in the early 20th century.

nobbut small, listen to the boatmen and you will discover which fish is at its best and even if you have to pay a bit extra it is always worth it.

Visitors along the quayside get to know what fresh fish looks like, but nothing about the life the fish lead in the wild, beneath the waves. Something of this hidden world can be understood by a visit to the Sea Life Centre in Scarborough. I was lucky enough to speak to the well-informed and articulate manager of the Centre, Richard Smith. We met in the car park with the waves of the North Sea sometimes splashing foam on the building itself. Richard told me,

All sea life centres concentrate on the marine life which exists in the area. This has always been the case since we opened in 1991.

Smacksmen gather for a 'crack' in Scarborough town, c.1890.

First of all you should see what I call the 'dump tanks', which direct volumes of seawater into our exhibits. Here waves are created and provide a natural habitat for the fish that keeps them healthy. There are only a couple of variations to conditions faced by fish in the wild. Firstly we obviously exclude predators, and we also feed the fish and take care to remove any discarded debris. Otherwise we leave the fish to enjoy their lives and at the same time give visitors a chance to take a view into the deep. There are rock pools containing crabs and lobsters, as well as shellfish, starfish and sea anemones. We do also enjoy taking part in conservation work. When one of our conger eels was ready to spawn, we located an old wreck out to sea and released the eel to join others in this ideal habitat. We have also released fish and, in association with government departments, placed tags prior to the release. In time this will allow us to monitor such features as growth rates and life spans. I always encourage our visitors to follow up their time with us with a trip to the harbour to look at the fish for sale.

I returned to the harbour early the following morning and met Stan Todhope, who was the chef of the Mount Hotel situated close to the Spa Conference Centre. Stan told me, 'I've been lucky this morning. I've managed to buy some scallops which are like very large cockles but are locally called queenies.'

Stan invited me to visit his kitchen and see and taste his recipe for queenies:

People often forget that inshore fishermen hereabout do not just catch fish but also sell crabs, lobsters, mussels and queenies. With modern communications as they are, most of these succulent items find their way onto the Continent and especially to France and Spain. To chefs like me this is a shame. Anyway, that's enough moaning. Let me prepare some queenies fit for a king! The secret of any shellfish is to be sure not to overcook it or spoil the taste with far too many ingredients. You should keep it simple. Firstly, put a mixture of butter and oil into a pan. Then chop just a little bacon and a touch of garlic. Soak the queenies in lemon juice with a touch of salt and black pepper. Place the lot into the butter and oil and add just a touch of white wine and a dressing of fresh cream. You should remember that this does not take long to cook and all you need to do is to enjoy it.

I certainly did enjoy this locally-sourced treat. This reminded me of one of the trips I made aboard the *Pentland Wave*. At one point we hove to alongside a fishing vessel and swapped a basket of queenies for a bottle of good Scotch whisky. Our on-board chef Elspeth rustled up a culinary treat which has never been equalled until Stan Todhope came up with this recipe.

Also with me on that *Pentland Wave* trip was botanist Dr Brian Barnes, who has since written books on the natural history of our coastline. Together we have led field trips, including some based at the Robin Hood Bay laboratory which has now closed. We followed this by concentrating our efforts around the North Yorkshire coast, especially around Scarborough and Filey. The relevance of this memory is that Brian Barnes is a gourmet and he made the point that most people, including chefs, know what seafood tastes like but know nothing about the biology of the things they are eating. 'It's a case of out of sight, out of mind', he went on. 'You're a zoologist, Ron, why don't you put pen to paper and put this right?'

It is almost ten years since Brian and I had that conversation and at last I've got round to fulfilling a little of what was suggested. The best known of the sea fish we eat is without doubt the cod. Until very recently it was the cheapest fish on the market and although it has become much more expensive, old habits die hard and people are reluctant to give up their cod and chips! A few years ago I visited the National Fishing Museum in Grimsby where the staff were known as the 'Cod Fathers'. The scientific name for the cod is *Gadus callarias* and when mature it is a very ugly fish due to its huge head and jaws; as it gets older it has a very pronounced 'pot belly'. When a fresh fish is examined, however, its greenish-brown body scales shine and also prominent are yellowish-brown spots. These colours are very attractive and so is the prominent white lateral line. The lateral line of a fish is full of tiny nerves which respond to water pressure and ensure that it can detect the movement of currents and that its body maintains its correct alignment.

Cod has long been a favourite with the British, not just because of its taste but because it can be caught in shallow waters from October until spring. During the summer months mature cod are found in deeper waters where they spawn. Cod are voracious feeders and prey on small fish but they do have a preference for herring. Because of their fierce feeding, cod grow very quickly and weigh over two pounds by the time they are two years old. It is because of their appetite that young cod are caught so often by shore-based anglers and these young fish make for excellent eating. Fish over 50 lbs in weight are often caught by trawlers and in parts of the Arctic, weights in excess of 200 lbs have been recorded. It is no wonder that trawlermen love the cod when huge fish help to swell their profits. The next time you visit a fishmonger's stall give some thought to the life histories of the species on offer. Invest in a relatively inexpensive fish book which will help to unravel the secrets of the deep.

When I joined a group of rod fishermen casting out from the beach at Scarborough, I met Clive Bennett, who told me,

I've always been a sea rod fisherman and my wife is a good cook so we have the best of both worlds. One of the best fish you can eat in our view is the little dabs. I've met lots of shore fishermen who won't eat dabs because they say that they are too small and too bony. This is because they don't know how to cook them reet and they don't know what they are missing. The taste is fantastic. My wife heads 'em and guts 'em and then poaches them in butter. She might add a sauce of shrimps with a dash of cream. She serves the dabs with small new potatoes soaked in butter and garden peas which we sometimes bring with us from our own allotment in Bradford. This is food to die for – I forget the cholesterol and ask for seconds!

The dab – scientific name *Limanda limanda* – is our smallest flat fish and related to the plaice, sole, halibut and turbot. The dab has a rough and dark upper surface whilst the lower surface is white. This makes sense because the dab lives close to the sandy seabed in shallow stretches. Seen from above some camouflage is essential to keep predators away but why waste the energy in producing defensive chemicals when your under surface is not seen! It is very unusual for dabs to weigh 2 lbs and most are much lighter than half a pound. I wrote down the recipe Clive Bennett gave me for dabs and it is now one of my favourites.

Not all fishmongers sell dabs although a few do, but it is better to talk to shore fishermen, keeping your wallet handy and prepare for a natter and a bargain hunt. You will often meet three generations of sea anglers here, with grandfathers passing on their skills to sons and grandsons. More and more women, too, are now rod fishing as I found out at Scarborough when I spoke briefly to Sophie Benson,

With all the mod cons we have today women are not tied to the wash tub and the stove and many of us share our husband's hobbies. I live in Scarborough now but I was born in Filey and all my mother's family were fishermen. They went out and still go out in cobles. This shows that we have Viking ancestors and if you are looking for memories of Yorkshire fishing you can't miss having a crack with the fisher folk at Filey.

Sophie was right and I well knew that my next port of call had to be along the coast to Filey.

Chapter 4

Filey

Although modern-day Filey is regarded as a rather refined seaside resort, thankfully, it still has one feature to delight the maritime historian. At the end of a comparatively new promenade is a very simple harbour populated by brightly-coloured painted cobles. They are moored there and look like multi-coloured whales left stranded on the beach by the tide. The boats are hauled up these days by tractor rather than by the sheer muscle power of brawny seamen.

Long before Hull was operating, Filey had an export trade extending as far as Portugal. Dried fish, especially skate wings, was much in demand in both Spain and Portugal. My first visit to Filey was in the mid 1980s after a friend had sent me a record made by the Filey Fishermen's Choir. Their repertoire proves that the fisherfolk hereabouts had long had a religious tradition. On the harbourside I met Jim Haxby, who told me,

I have been an inshore fisherman for nearly 50 years and I have followed in the footsteps of my father, grandfather and several generations before them. Our techniques for catching fish have changed very little over the years. Inshore fishermen like me regard ourselves as farmers of the sea and we operate at distances up to six miles out from the beach. From October to March we operate long-line fishing, mainly for cod and our hooks are usually baited with

Modern-day Filey is a delightful mix of a working fishing village and a holiday resort.

The coble landing at Filey has functioned as a fishing beach and an amusement area since Victorian times.

A rare shot of a flither girl, c.1900. These girls searched the rock pools of Filey for shellfish which they sold to line fishermen as bait.

mussels. There are people working on the mussel beds who also sell these shellfish, which are good to eat providing they are cooked reet. From 1st June to 31st August we operate a small salmon boat. We really do have to be good at this job if the boat is to earn its keep because apart from the cost of diesel, the salmon licence is increasingly expensive and in excess of £1,000. From March onwards as the sea temperature reaches above 6°C we can start to fish for crabs and lobsters. We can operate our pots until the end of September when the cod is literally on-line again.

Jim proved to me that all commercial fishing involves a combination of art and science. When I was a student, my professor told me that if I wanted to understand the biology of our coastline I first had to visit a fishing harbour, look out for an ancient mariner and be prepared to learn. I have never forgotten that and Jim Haxby was very like a vocal textbook for anyone interested in the memories of the fishing industry. He continued,

We fish every day unless the weather makes it impossible. I reckon that four days gives us our running expenses and the extra days make up our profits. Strong easterly winds are a disaster on this coast and we like south westerlies when we can fish in conditions up to a force six or even seven. Even though we are properly dressed, high winds and waves give us a good wetting but you can bring in good catches. You mentioned our boats which, as you know, we call cobles and they are totally based on the Viking design. When we say they are clinker-built, all this means is that the boat is made of overlapping planks which obviously keep out the water. Our boats are heavier than they used to be because of the weight of the diesel engine, but I can remember during the war when my grandfather was teaching me to fish and he always preferred to use sail power. To get our cobles up and down the beach in them days the fishermen employed retired fishermen and horses to do the work. Obviously my generation prefers using diesel power and a good tractor but I still remember these tough old days with affection. In bad weather navigation was a real problem before we had so many electronic aids and the old timers told me that they relied on the church bells of St Oswald's which were rung in bad weather, especially in fog, and which guided them home.

As already mentioned, fishermen have always been a religious breed which is not surprising as they risk very close contact with their Maker every time they face the sea. It is fitting that the weather vane atop the church tower is in the shape of a fish, which has been the symbol of Christianity since its birth. Christianity and fishing have long been linked and this is proved by the impressive history of the Filey Fishermen's Choir. This originated from its Methodist roots in 1823 when it was founded by John Oxtoby. By 1865 it had so many members that a new building was constructed to cope with the number. The choir has long had connections with

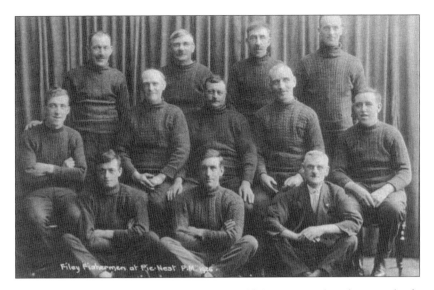

Jim Haxby's family come from a long line of fishermen. In this photograph of the Filey Fishermen's Choir in 1926, Matt Haxby is first left on the back row.

the Haxby family; Matt Haxby was in the choir in 1926 and Jim continues to exercise his vocal chords to this day.

I had a tape of the choir playing in my car whilst waiting to meet James McKenzie, who was then an ambitious young chef, on his way to the coble landing to buy a couple of crabs which he had arranged to cook for me as part of one of the BBC radio programmes I was making. In the warmth of his kitchen, full of fascinating sounds and smells, James told me,

Crabs is o'reet – it just depends on how you cooks 'em. I boil 'em for about 20 minutes and then take the claws off and extract the meat from the shell. You have to take out a black bit called dead men's fingers. Some people say this is poisonous but it isn't, it just doesn't taste good and is quite bitter. There are two sorts of crab flesh, one much darker than the other. Some won't eat the dark flesh but I think it tastes better. What I do is to wrap the flesh between two pieces of filo pastry and the colour is not immediately apparent in the parcel. I use plenty of butter between the sheets of filo and the crab flesh and add plenty of salt, black pepper and lemon juice.

James served this dish with a light parsley sauce after placing the 'parcel' in an oven at 220°C for about 10 minutes. He added a vinaigrette sauce with olive oil and served it with fresh, locally-grown vegetables. I visited James on another occasion when he gave me another crab meal, this time served in a pasta sauce.

Throughout my research for this book, I have been delighted to discover just how cheaply the old fishing families, who also had their own allotments, could live. They were pretty well self-sufficient. I did want to pursue the history of Filey, though, and I met up with Michael Feron who has studied the history of the town in some depth. He told me,

Filey is only 7 miles along the coast from Scarborough. Back in the 8th century and almost certainly long before that, it made its living from farming and fishing. There is a 12th-century manuscript relating to a fishing conflict. The monasteries of Lincoln and Whitby both owned lands in the Filey area and demanded tithes from the fisherfolk. This proves that there must have been good fishing even then but the locals cannot have been too pleased when two abbeys tried to tax them at the same time.

Michael told me that in the 19th century Filey had some famous visitors and one was the composer Frederick Delius (1862–1934) who was born in Bradford. His family were well-off and made their fortune from the wool trade and they spent long summer holidays in Filey. Young Frederick played cricket for the local teams but loved fishing and often went out with the boatmen in their cobles.

A brief mention should be made of Butlin's Holiday Camp, which was in the process of being built in 1939 when the war came. The camp was requisitioned and it was here that the RAF Regiment was first formed. What was once the parade ground was later flooded to produce a boating lake. After the war Butlin's completed the

Fishing for mackerel off Filey Brigg has been a popular pastime for many years.

self-sufficient holiday camp, which was at its peak in the 1950s and 1960s. Alice Ramsbottom of Bolton remembers this well,

> *During our wakes holidays we always went to Butlin's at Filey. In 1957 I were ten but two of my brothers were older. I went on the fairground – you paid one fee and everything was then free so there were no need to spend owt – but my brothers were working. They saved up and went out with the boatmen on the coble landing to fish and got seasick. They became friends with the fisherfolk and long after they were married they got lodgings near the quayside and fished and took their kids to search in the rock pools.*

Michael Feron put me in touch with Margaret Wilkins, who was the curator of the Filey Museum on Queens Street. Margaret is another very careful historian and she gave me a guided tour of seven rooms which had been converted from a couple of old fishermen's cottages. The first room was devoted to the history of

Women knitting ganzies on Bridlington harbour, 1890.

This unique photograph, c.1890, shows a collection of fishermen wearing ganzies from their home ports, including Staithes, Robin Hood's Bay, Scarborough, Filey and Bridlington.

the fishing industry and the lifeboats. Margaret told me the story of the 'ganzies', which are patterned pullovers,

> *Each fishing village had its own knitted pattern and this helped identification in the sad times when the body of a drowned fisherman was picked up on a remote beach months after he had perished. There are just a few ladies left who can still knit our Filey pattern.*

I have a personal memory of the ganzie as my maternal grandmother, who was born in Northumberland, had spent some of her early life in Whitby. I have followed her example and my family still refer to our pullovers as ganzies.

Margaret Wilkins went on to tell me of the early history of the lifeboat service at Filey,

> *We do have memories here of the lifeboat service, including a device which fired maroons to call the men to the lifeboat in the days before telephones, mobile phones and other electronic devices of the modern age. In those days most, if not all, of the lifeboat crews were working or retired fisherfolk who were born and bred in the area, with sea water in their blood.*

From Margaret I made my way back towards the coble landing to speak to Malcolm Johnson, who was then the assistant coxswain of the lifeboat. He told me,

> *All the early lifeboats were based on the very sturdy and seaworthy Viking longships which are still being used here at the coble landing. Their design meant that those boats could work from the shores in the days before purpose-built harbours became common. These clinker-built wooden boats worked really well and our modern day vessels have retained the basic shape but when oar and sail were replaced by diesel they were obviously much heavier. Our present boat is made of very strong and chemically complicated plastics and now bristles with electronic devices. She also has an enclosed*

cabin which keeps the crew dry except when they are working on deck during a rescue. What has not changed is that our boat is still launched from the beach. These days she is hauled up and down the back by means of a very powerful tractor.

We still get plenty of willing volunteers but with fewer and fewer fishermen operating out of Filey the crew is more of a mixed bunch and made up of schoolteachers, paramedics and others. They all carry pagers and when these are activated they rush to the assembly point. It is not now the first to arrive who go out but the coxswain who chooses seven. This selection is largely based on what the potential disaster is predicted to be. If there are likely to be injuries, then a paramedic is the first to be chosen. The boat now has direct communications with all the other emergency services, including an air ambulance. If you will forgive the pun, lifeboat crews these days are not 'cobbled' together as they were in the old days but are equipped to conduct very complex and sophisticated rescue missions.

Malcolm was too modest to mention one aspect which has been part of the lifeboat service from its very beginnings and that is the dedication and bravery of the crew. Connie Riley, who lived in Scarborough for most of her life, put this point very well,

All of my mother's family had been fisherfolk since at least 1840. From 1890 to 1930 two of my uncles combined fishing with crewing the lifeboats all along the Yorkshire coast. All fishermen compete hard to deliver the best-filled nets or hook the most fish, but when their competitors were in trouble all rivalries were forgotten except to wage war against the sea.

Chapter 5

Bridlington

Bridlington, by far the largest of the coastal resorts of the old East Riding of Yorkshire, is too often dismissed as merely another 19th-century tourist town. Actually Old Bridlington was built a little distance inland and around the parish church of St Mary which dates back to the time when it was a monastic priory.

Fishing in Bridlington takes us back, as with Whitby, Scarborough and Filey, as well as the villages in between, at least to Anglo-Saxon times but obviously documentary evidence is scarce. There is, however, archaeological evidence in the form of middens which indicate that the bounty from the sea and shore was gratefully accepted. From the foundation of Bridlington's Augustinian priory in 1113, the brethren held the fishing rights. They built a small fishing pier and the prior also served as the harbour master. It seems certain that the monks employed men to fish from the Viking-based cobles. When Henry VIII dissolved the priory in 1535 he left the chapel to become the parish church but he destroyed the rest of the extensive complex, with the surprising exception of the Bayle Gate. This was probably the main entrance to the abbey and is now a museum. Stone from the priory ruins was used to construct new harbour walls, as well as other buildings in the town.

The old quay was originally separated from the priory town but the space between the two has gradually been built upon. On the north side is a museum of harbour history containing a

Bridlington harbour in the late 19th century.

graphic display dealing with the evolution of fishing methods. It is open during the season. The North Sea is notoriously stormy and dangerous and the brave men manning the lifeboat station have always been busy along this stretch of coastline; the Bridlington Lifeboat House situated on South Marine Drive is also worth an extended visit.

By the 18th century, Bridlington was a thriving port and there were also rich merchants making good livings. Among the most prominent were members of the Graham family whose home base was at Sewerby Hall. I spoke to the curator of this splendid building. Niall Adams told me,

We know that there was an old manor house on this site in the 14th century but most historians suggest that it was occupied much earlier than this and possibly as early as Anglo-Saxon times. There are accounts to show that fish has always been important in the diet of the residents of the Manor. In 1709 the Graham family first rented Sewerby and in 1714 they had sufficient funds to purchase the estate consisting of the house and 50 acres of land. The Grahams were in residence until 1934 when they sold the whole estate to Bridlington Council who were at first more interested in the gardens than the house. The views down into the harbour with the boats bobbing about in the water are spectacular. Close by is an Anglo-Saxon cemetery which proves that there was a substantial settlement at this time.

From Sewerby the 400-ft-high chalk cliffs of Bempton are a good place to visit and the history of the 'climmers' is fascinating, as I found out when I spoke to ornithologist Athol Wallis,

For six weeks during the summer, the eggs of the guillemot were in demand by gourmets. From the 1850s when the railway came the market generated by the cities was insatiable and the climmers

Pleasure boats in Bridlington harbour in the 1950s.

55

earned a good living. Fishermen and farm workers could earn four times as much from the egg trade. The men worked in teams of four with three strong men lowering one brave man down ropes and onto the cliff edge. Fishermen were particularly good at this job because they knew ropes and movements generated by the wind. Guillemots lay the largest egg compared with the size of the bird than any other British species. The climmers also noted that the female birds always lay eggs of the same pattern from birth to death and can live for more than 20 years. Even though only one egg is laid the climmers discovered that the birds who had their eggs pinched would lay a second and third egg and so no damage was done to the population. Despite this, climming declined and had disappeared by the 1950s.

Athol was fulsome in his praise of the climmers' skill and bravery but he pointed out that the best way to see the bird colonies was from the sea. This meant that I had to pay a visit to Bridlington harbour where I met Peter Richardson, who operates pleasure boats. He told me,

We work very closely with the fishermen and my two boats are largely crewed by men who have a great knowledge of the sea and many learned their skills as a result of inshore fishing. I operate two pleasure boats during the tourist season. The Flamborian *was built in 1938 and the* Yorkshire Belle *was launched in 1947. Both were built in Beverley. They have lots of character and our longer trips go as far as Flamborough Head. There is live music on board, including sea shanties – proof that fishermen and indeed all sailors sing in a rhythm which helps them to do their work when hauling nets.*

I returned from a bracing trip aboard the *Flamborian*, with live music still ringing in my ears, and met a fisherman who had saved me a monkfish, which I took to the Sea Court Hotel where I met the chef, Philip Brewer. The monkfish must be one of the ugliest of British fishes. Philip told me:

Don't worry about the huge gaping mouth because I cut this off and the tasty bits are the body and the tail. I always specialise in fish and visit the market every morning to see what is on offer. All the local chefs have their favourite fishermen and they actually compete with each other to offer us the best catch of the day. Nobody would dream of cheating because discerning customers like us vote with our feet. I'll cook you your monkfish but just for once do not drink wine with it but select a good quality beer.

Philip Brewer was an ideal name for him, but he pointed out to me a plaque on the wall of the bar which reads,

May the Lord Above send down a dove
With wings as sharp as razors,
To cut the throats of all those blokes
Who sell bad beer to sailors.

Inshore fishermen examining their catch.

The last word on Bridlington has to be from Steve Sawyer, who was once Tourism Officer for the town. He was born and bred in the place that he still loves,

Catching fish is one thing but selling it is quite another. There has been a fish market here even probably before the monks. The coming of the railways in the 1850s was a real boost and fish could be exported all over inland Yorkshire and beyond. It was during this period that what is now the huge city of Hull expanded and dominated the fishing industry of Yorkshire.

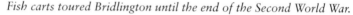

Fish carts toured Bridlington until the end of the Second World War.

Chapter 6

Hull

In the Beginning

Like all ports, Hull had a modest beginning. In the 12th century there was only a small trading centre called Wyke which developed at the point where the River Hull flows into the Humber. The word *wyke* is Old English in origin and simply means a settlement based around a dairy farm but there seems to be no doubt that from Viking times onwards there was a small fishing fleet similar to that at Filey. Trade at this little port increased so much that Edward I (1272–1307) renamed it Kingston-upon-Hull and granted it a Charter of Incorporation. With powerful royal backing, Hull developed to such an extent that, by the 18th century, wharves and warehouses had been constructed and prosperous shipowners and merchants were building impressive Georgian mansions.

For some time, the production of grain was important and large volumes were exported. As the Industrial Revolution gathered pace, iron goods and textiles were sent all over the world, but especially to Russia and the Baltic. Gradually, Hull evolved into a major whaling port, with ships venturing out into distant waters in search of the valuable oil.

Alexandra Dock. Hull.

Alexandra Dock, c.1910.

Until the mid 19th century the fishing industry in Hull played second fiddle to the whaling and the main East Coast fishery was based at Scarborough. Apart from the inshore fleet, those vessels venturing further afield were mainly manned by Dutch sailors using fishing smacks built at Brixham in Devon, which was famous for its mackerel fishery.

It seems that in 1864 one of these Scarborough vessels was driven into the Humber estuary by a storm and had its nets torn to pieces. One substantial but very tattered segment of net was hauled in and found to have caught substantial numbers of sole. This species then, as now, was a luxury item and commanded a high price. The crew realised that they had literally been blown across a lucrative fishing ground and they applied a searching technique which would be the envy of a modern forensic scientist. They plotted their unscheduled journey and eventually found what became known as the Silver Pit, which is about 70 miles to the east of Spurn Head. So prolific was the area that Brixham owners moved many of their vessels to take advantage of this bonus and by 1855 they had taken over a small corner of Hull docks. They made such good profits, helped by a developing railway network, that boats were attracted from as far away as Portsmouth, Ramsgate and Barking Creek, on the banks of the River Thames, whilst the bulk of the Scarborough fleet was also relocated to Hull.

In retrospect it would seem that Scarborough missed an opportunity to develop into a prosperous trawling port. When the Brixham fishermen discovered the sole, they wanted to land their catch in Scarborough but the local inshore men did not take kindly to this competition and fierce fights developed using knives as well as fists. The Brixham men opted for the quieter haven which was Hull.

The essential space needed to land increasingly large catches, as well as providing berths for ever more vessels, came very much at a premium. This led some merchants to move across the Humber and establish a rival fishing port at Grimsby, the latter with the advantage of not having to compete for space with the well-established whaling fleet which was then dominating Hull. Hull reacted in 1869 by building the Albert Dock specifically for the

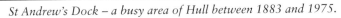

St Andrew's Dock – a busy area of Hull between 1883 and 1975.

fishing fleet but even this proved unable to cope with demand and St Andrew's Dock was built in 1883.

The best place to begin an exploration of Hull is around the marina. Although this concentrates these days on luxury cruisers, there is a floating museum close by, open throughout the year, based on board the Spurn lightship, built at Goole in 1927 at a cost of £17,000. The vessel was firmly moored about 4 miles off the Spurn lighthouse at the head of the Humber and was much loved by the trawlermen on their way home after a tough but hopefully prosperous voyage.

Benjamin Wilkes who recalls the time when his grandfather worked aboard the Spurn lightship.

I found out more about the lightship thanks to my godmother Doris Dickinson, whose father was at one time a port missionary in Hull. Doris put me in touch with Benjamin Wilkes, whose maternal grandfather spent some time aboard the Spurn lightship and who was brim full of facts and figures,

The vessel had no engines but was towed into the correct location and then secured in position by huge anchors, which were needed in these stormy waters. Spare anchors were carried and there was a crew of four who stayed on station for a month at a time. There was a master, an engineer to service the light and batteries for lighting. There was a cook and an odd job man who were always kept busy. There were five lightships around the Humber, the other four being the Bull and the Lower, Middle and Upper Whitton lights. I remember Mr Dickinson very well and for a time the religious fellas were based on a boat which was called the Prayer Packet.

The lightships were used as part of a defensive boom across the Humber during the Second World War, when Hull was among the most heavily bombed cities in Britain and was also under threat of attacks from the sea. In May 1946 the Spurn lightship was returned to her original berth and there was a replacement and refitting in 1959, with her black and white hull repainted red and placed on station at Bull. In 1979 she was decommissioned and would have rotted away had she not been bought by Hull City Council in 1983 and opened as a museum in 1987. This was at a time when the fishing trawlers at Grimsby and Hull were enjoying a boom period, as skipper Derek Keetley recalls,

Every man jack of us loved the lightships. In bad weather the lights flashed to a unique pattern and there was also a foghorn which boomed out the same pattern. This ensured that we knew just where we were. Even during later times when we had a mass of electronic communications, the sight and especially the sound of this vessel was like a homecoming call.

Benjamin Wilkes records the memories on the other side of the partnership and he told me,

> *These vessels were virtually unsinkable as the designers constructed them of strong steel divided by watertight bulkheads and each compartment was self-contained. Each could be individually sealed off if an emergency arose. The vital structure, of course, was the lantern tower. Lightships were just extensions of the time when prominent buildings ashore were used to warn mariners that land and dangerous rocks were too close for comfort. As early as 1428 a chap called Richard Readbarrow had erected a beacon close to Spurn Head and, in 1776, John Smeaton built the Spurn lighthouse. In 1820 the idea of a 'floating light' was suggested, along with a proposed toll of one farthing per ton to contribute to the maintenance. It was, however, only in 1832 that the Bull lightship came on station but this was not very successful as it was made of wood. As early as 1847 the wooden lightship was replaced by one of iron.*

By 1927 the lightships were very comfortable for the crew and the vessel now on view makes it possible to appreciate how they worked, cooked and rested, as well as keeping in touch with their shore base. These days, lightships are not manned, as remote electronically-operated equipment is used. George Burns regrets this change,

> *I know that I have to move with the times but in this modern world we tend not to talk to people but email them or keep in contact by Twitter and Facebook. I remember working as a trawlerman out of Hull in the 1950s and after a rough trip and coming home in bad weather we made a point of visiting the families of lighthouse and lightship keepers to give the ladies of those fellas a packet of fish which we had as part of our wages. In good weather we could wave at these chaps on duty and shout thanks to them for keeping us safe.*

Chapter 7

Whaling in Hull

By far the best place to start discovering the impressive maritime history of Hull is at the Town Docks Museum in Queen Victoria Square. The museum dominates the city centre and the building it is housed in was built in 1871 to accommodate the offices of the Hull Dock Company. It fulfilled this function until the early 1970s. Graphically covered in the museum is the history of the fishing industry, including whaling and the natural history of these marine mammals.

At first, mariners thought whales were just big fish and this is why I consider the industry to be very relevant to this book. There is no doubt that early hunters made no distinction between whales and large fish, particularly sharks, but eventually it was realised that the former had warm blood, breathed atmospheric air through a pair of lungs and the females fed their young on milk delivered via mammary glands.

Then came the scientists, eager to classify animals and invent long names. Marine mammals, whales and dolphins were placed in the order *cetacae*, made up of around 80 species, many of which are now very much under threat. Most belong to the sub-order *odontoceti* or toothed whales and the rest to the sub-order *mysticeti*, more commonly known as the baleen or whalebone whales. The *odontoceti* are carnivores and include killer and pilot whales and dolphins. Nineteenth-century scientists were very able

The Diana *was the last whaler to operate out of Hull.*

anatomists and when the whaling industry was in full swing they had a constant flow of specimens. They soon noticed that apart from having teeth, the *odontoceti* had their skull bones arranged asymmetrically and only one breathing or blow hole leading to a branch into each of the two lungs.

Members of this sub-order are, comparatively speaking, small and apart from the sperm whales (the *odontoceti*) were not hunted by the whaling fleets, which obviously went in search of the much larger plankton-feeding members of the *mysticeti*. The Americans, however, hunted sperm whales and Moby Dick was a member of this species. They produce very rich oil which is stored within the head area. This is shaped rather like a melon. The fluid changes from solid to liquid at 31°C which is the whale's body temperature. As it dives after squid, the cold deep water changes the liquid oil to a solid fat and thus alters the buoyancy of the animal.

Instead of teeth, the *mysticeti* have a system of horn-like plates through which they filter their food. These plates are known as whalebone or baleen and, as we shall see later, were just as valuable as the oil. Baleen is composed of keratin, the same substance which makes up our own hair and nails. It is very light and like hair and nails grows continually to replace that which is worn away. The plates allow the whale to extract huge volumes of plankton, known as krill, from the water. Baleen whales also have grooves in the area of the throat, and such structures are lacking in the toothed whales. The skull bones of the *mysticeti* are symmetrical and they have two blow holes, each of which leads into a lung. There are three families, namely the *balaenopteridae* which includes the rorquals, an Old Norwegian word for 'grooves', the *balaenidae* or right whales and the *eschrichtiidae* or grey whales, represented by only one very important species. Amongst members of the rorquals are the blue whale, the largest animal in the world and the humpbacked whale, which has an easily recognised shape. The naming of the right whales came about as they are considered to be the 'right whales' to hunt from small boats because they swim so slowly that they can be easily caught and harpooned.

Such huge animals could only have evolved in the sea where the water supports the immense weight of the body. Blue whales can reach a length of around 30 metres and weigh more than 130 tonnes and it can be seen why just one catch brought enormous profit. Whales propel themselves by moving the tail up and down which is in contrast to fish which move their tail from side to side. Whales can, however, occasionally move their tails sideways and this gives them extra manoeuvrability. The dorsal fin acts as a stabiliser.

The presence of body hair would also be a problem to a marine animal and in the absence of the usual mammalian insulator, the maintenance of body temperature presented an evolutionary problem. Nature's answer was blubber. This thick insulating layer of fat beneath the skin was largely responsible for the development of commercial whaling.

No doubt early civilisations came in contact with *cetacaens* which were washed ashore dead or dying and such a huge supply of meat must have been most welcome. A beached whale soon dies because once the support of the water has been lost, the sheer weight of the body tissues crushes the lungs and leads to suffocation.

It was with beached animals that the history of whaling began, and there is some archaeological evidence to show that the bodies were cut up using stone tools which have been found close to piles of bones. The carcass provided food but the bones were also used to make furniture and also to support buildings. The oil was used for lighting and for cooking. This bonanza from the sea was still much valued in England as early as 1324 when a law was passed by Edward II which stipulated that any beached *cetacaen* belonged to the Crown. At this time much of western France was under the control of England and the Basques on the Bay of Biscay paid a bounty to England for each beached whale. The British monarch's right has now passed to the Natural History Museum in London whose collection over the years has prospered because of it.

There can be no doubt that primitive people felt that waiting for the valuable animals to beach themselves could be speeded up if they put to sea and tried to drive the whales ashore. Pilot whales were the favoured prey and the people of Shetland were driving as late as 1903. The inhabitants of the Faroes still attract the anger of conservationists by continuing the rituals of this bloody slaughter. Some were even brave enough to paddle after whales with harpoons, but they did not kill enough to have any effect at all on the populations. The same cannot be said of later European and American whalers who cared not for food or for the comfort of the crew but only for profits. Men went in headlong pursuit of the larger species.

Historians believe that it was in the Basque area of the Bay of Biscay that an initial 'whale drive' led to the pursuit of quarry further and further out to sea, with the main species killed being the baleen black right whale. In the early days the carcass was still towed back to the beach for the cutting up process which is known as flensing. The whales in the Basque area feed mainly on immature sardines which are common in the Bay of Biscay. The Basque towns of Fuenterrabia, Bermeo and Biarritz still feature whales on their coats of arms. Some historians have suggested that the Basques may have learned their techniques from Norwegians, who are known to have traded in the area. There are written records compiled for Alfred of Wessex telling of Norwegian whalers in the late 9th century.

By the late 16th and early 17th centuries the whaling ships were reaching as far as Newfoundland where the black right whales were common. Here they also caught fish, especially cod, which they dried or salted for the return journey. Ice-carrying trawlers were still a long way in the future.

The year 1553 was a significant date in the annals of British whaling as Hugh Willoughby set off in a vain effort to find a north-eastern trade passage to China, thus avoiding passing through seas dominated by Arab pirates. He failed to find the passage but did reach Archangel and set up the Muscovy Company. One of the enterprises which this company developed was whaling but initially the English did not have the expertise required to chase, harpoon, kill and process whales. They therefore employed Basques and in time copied their methods; the classic form of industrial espionage. Henry Hudson also tried to find the trade passage during 1607 and 1608 and although he also failed he was able to report a great abundance of whales and marked their positions and concentrations on maps. In 1610 John Poole charted the island of Spitsbergen and one area in particular was marked Whale Bay.

Whale fever was now well and truly on and the Muscovy Company fitted out two vessels: the *Elizabeth*, which belonged to Thomas Poole, and the *Margaret*. Although the two vessels were ill-fated they did herald the start of the British whaling industry and Hull was involved from the beginning, albeit by accident. The two vessels killed and processed thirteen right whales but the *Margaret* sailed too close to the ice and was slowly crushed. Her cargo was transferred to the *Elizabeth* but it was so badly stored that she eventually capsized. A Hull vessel called the *Hopewell* was in the area fishing further north than was usual in those days and she took off both crews and a portion of their catch. Once this arrived 'home' a new industry quickly evolved as whale oil was much in demand for lamps prior to the discovery of coal gas, petroleum and electricity.

In its time whale oil has been used for very many other purposes including the manufacture of tallow, soap, glycerine (which was the basis of the nitro-glycerine explosive industry), tanning, machine oil, oil paints and the grease to prevent the snapping of textile threads. The oil from the sperm whale was especially valuable and is still (alas) in demand today for lubricating oils, scouring agents and especially cosmetics. This has brought whaling countries such as Norway, Japan and Iceland into conflict with other countries and especially conservationists who feel that there are plenty of alternatives available.

Another product once dependent upon the baleen whales was the so-called whalebone. This was immersed in hot water which made it pliable enough to be moulded into corsets, fishing rods, brushes for chimney sweeps and springs for machinery.

Other European countries and later the Americans also had greedy eyes on the trade and minor wars were fought over the whaling grounds. The initial battles were fought between the Dutch and the Muscovy Company which was soon wound up but superseded by the Greenland Company. In the period 1612–1618, really serious fighting took place. A tentative political settlement was reached in 1618 in which the best whaling grounds were divided between the Basque, Spanish, Hamburg, Dutch, Danish and English fleets. At first the Dutch were the dominant whalers, but ships from York and Hull were already working by 1650. These whalers were soon joined by a substantial fleet from Whitby.

Once a commodity becomes freely available, it is amazing how many uses are found for it and, by the 18th century, whale oil was used as a substitute for the expensive tallow in the production of cheap soap and was also used to treat wool prior to spinning. The resultant cloth was somewhat rough but, as almost the whole of Europe was at war during the period up to 1815, there was an almost insatiable demand for cheap uniforms. After the peace, ladies' fashions quickly evolved and the 'hour-glass' shape was achieved by the fierce application of 'string and whalebone' corsets. Peace in Europe meant the return to a lively nightlife and many streets and buildings were lit by burning whale oil which produced little smoke but a very bright flame. The demand for more and more oil meant the establishment of whaling stations on Greenland to which the carcasses were taken for processing. Stocks of whales quickly diminished and the stations were deserted as the ships became large enough to process the catch on board and pushed further and further into the ice packs.

The profits of whaling around Greenland were often considerable, but the possibility of failure was ever present. Even the capture of one large whale, however, could cover the cost of a voyage and there are records of one ship killing 50 whales during a season. In 1748 the British industry received a boost from the government which saw whalers as ideal training grounds for seamen who could be drafted directly into the navy in the event of war. They agreed to pay £1 for each ton of whaling ship and this was doubled in 1750. The owners were also given £50 for each of their boats capable of chasing whales.

A visit to the Town Docks Museum in Hull should not be rushed as it is possible to trace the history of whaling by strolling around its galleries. Here are artefacts ranging from the primitive methods employed by the Eskimos to the sophisticated techniques used on board a modern whaler. There is also a comprehensive collection of surprisingly clear photographs depicting the whole grizzly process.

In the early days, when a whale was sighted, a rowing boat was lowered with the harpooner up front waiting his chance to hurl his metal javelin into the flesh of the whale which then dived, as so graphically described by the American Herman Melville (1810–1891) in his novel *Moby Dick*. The word 'harpoon' comes from the Basque word *arpoi* but some historians think that the root is from the French *harper*, which means 'to grapple', a good description for this crude and cruel weapon.

The chase was certainly bloody, painful and often a fatal exercise. Obviously this was the case for the whale but also quite often for its hunters. Stowing the harpoon and its attached rope in the confines of a small boat was a skill in itself and as the whale dived it took with it the harpoon and several hundred feet of rope. Emergency food, water, a mast, sails, oars, hatchets, boat-hooks and grapples were also carefully stowed. The whale, being an

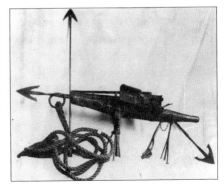

Harpoon gun, c.1830.

air breather, had to surface, when the waiting harpooner hoped to hurl another dart in the hope of striking a vital organ. In any case the whale became weaker and weaker and as its strength ebbed, the harpooner wrapped his rope around a specially strengthened pillar in the boat called a stave or a bollard. The rope could be wound in or paid out as required. If the whale regained strength, the rope could unwind so quickly that it became hot with friction and had to be doused with water. Eventually the whale died and its carcass was taken either to the shore factory or to a specially adapted ship.

Flensing at a shore-based station was hard work although technically easy, but to carry out the operation even in a calm sea was a much more difficult proposition. Firstly the whale had to be tied up alongside the ship with its head facing the stern. Once this was done two rowing boats were pushed in close to the whale, thus sandwiching its body. Then the men, called krengers, who often wore spiked boots, clambered onto the body and began to cut it up using long and very sharp knives. This would have been a most dangerous operation when there was a heavy sea running and flat calm waters must have been the exception rather than the rule. Huge blocks of blubber were cut and lifted by crude cranes onto the deck. They were dropped on the starboard side of the ship and the blubber was stripped from the skin and chopped into pieces. These were pushed down a chute made of sail canvas into a barrel which was then sealed. Once the flesh had been taken off, the baleen 'bone' was removed and packed into the hold.

An effort was made on some vessels to process the blubber instead of carrying the decaying mess to a home port, but this was not without its dangers. Most of the shore-based operations could be duplicated but the 'tryworks' was a real problem. This was a huge copper boiler mounted on a brick furnace and on which blubber was heated to drive out the 'train oil', the first word deriving from the Dutch word for a tear drop. It probably got this name because the oil oozes out in bubbles from the flesh. European whalers were terrified of the fires which could be caused by the tryworks but, as most of their whaling was carried out in the cold Arctic, the barrels of untreated blubber could be easily transported. The

The art of scrimshaw – here is depicted the London registered whaler, Ranger.

American vessels on the other hand often travelled further south, even down into the Antarctic, and passed through warmer areas. They therefore had to process their blubber on board. They erected tryworks amidships, set on top of a deep tray of water. This may well have worked because there are no records of any major disaster.

By the time they had made their kill, the men may have been continually on the hunt for several days in an open boat and in constant danger of being thrown into the water. During the long voyages to and from the killing grounds the sailors must have watched the other forms of life in the Arctic and many had a great deal of artistic talent. They developed a unique art form by scratching pictures onto baleen. This is called scrimshaw and the Town Docks Museum has a fine collection of this work. It is often a wonderfully accurate portrait of the wildlife, obviously including whales, but with birds and other mammals well represented. Men being men, the fairer sex is also featured and any other aspect of life which was exercising the mind of the artist at the time. The whalers probably picked up the technique from the Eskimos who decorated the teeth, bones and tusks of the walrus and any other suitable material left over from their blubbery feasts.

Alex Winchester, whose family worked in several fishing ports, told me,

Lots of my wife's family were whalers and we still have examples of their artistic work which is known as scrimshaw. I even met a man whose name was Jacob Scrimshaw. Scrimshaw was a real skill and whaling men spent their off-duty hours carving whalebone into ornaments which are now of great value. You should remember that whaling differed from fishing in the sense that they did not have to haul nets but were really only busy when chasing whales. Most whaling companies had stations based on remote islands around the Arctic.

These whaling stations were used by German U-boats during the Second World War, as I discovered when writing *Yorkshire – The Secret War* (Countryside Books, 2010). The records of the 18th- and 19th-century whaling companies were carefully scrutinised by the Admiralty during the battle of the Atlantic.

Audrey Mill, whom I met whilst working in Australia, discovered that her ancestors were whalers and told me,

When I was speaking to you, I realised that we had some old bones with carvings on them which my father gave me before he died in 1986. He emigrated to Australia in the 1950s and among his family possessions were these bones as he called them. I now know that they are good examples of scrimshaw work.

Audrey wrote to me in 2010 and told me that she now could trace her father's ancestry back to 1839 when he lived in Hull and worked as a mariner. He was obviously employed in the whaling fleet.

The Hull museum also has a collection of whaling machinery, including the evolution of the modern harpoon gun. It was neither safe nor efficient for the harpooners to attack the largest of whales and they were often unsuccessful although the rewards were so great that it did not stop them trying. The giants often took a long time to die and then sank very soon afterwards. Once a harpoon gun had been invented and mounted in the bow of a steam ship the door was opened to the large-scale slaughter of whales, leading inevitably to their present demise. It is hard for us to realise how common whales once were around the coastlines of most countries in the world although they were probably always more numerous in the plankton-rich waters around the poles.

The first guns simply discharged a barbed harpoon attached to a length of rope into the whale, to be followed by more and more harpoons until the animal died or a lucky shot severed a vital nerve or blood vessel. Svend Foyn, a Norwegian mariner, was experimenting with whaling during the 1870s and produced a harpoon with a delayed-action explosive charge which detonated some seconds after entering the whale. He also invented a device to absorb the shock placed on the line as the stricken whale headed for the safety of the deep. As the whale was being winched in, the harpoon wound was sealed with a huge stopper and the body pumped full of air to keep it afloat.

As the northern whale stocks diminished, attention was turned to the Antarctic. South Georgia and the Falkland Islands were important in the development of the Antarctic whaling grounds during the late 19th and early 20th century.

In 2000, I interviewed Aaron Melville in Whitby who recalled some wonderful whaling memories,

I still get letters from American scholars trying to find out if I am related to the author of Moby Dick. *I'd love to think that I was but I have a family Bible dating to 1743 and it proves beyond doubt that I am not related to the author. What the Bible does show though is that the males in my family were whalers from 1786 to 1869 and then were trawlermen from 1872 to the 1970s when I retired from the sea. I have artefacts such as scrimshaw work done by a relative called Amos Melville who was a good but not an outstanding artist carving on whalebone. His grandson was a fisherman trawling out of Hull from the 1930s and went to war in a trawler in 1940.*

It was only when I was commissioned to write this book that I remembered to search in my diary of July 2000 to read of the graphic account provided by Aaron Melville, who died in 2001.

Obviously stories of whaling have been more difficult to collect than is the case with the trawlermen and fisherfolk of Hull, where memories are fresh. A remnant of what was once a mighty fleet survives and the fish auctions are still a feature of the town.

I have been interested in the history of fishing for most of my life and I have been lucky enough to meet with Lionel Marr on many occasions. He told me,

My family have been involved in trawling since it first began but there would not have been a fishing industry had there not been a whaling fleet based in Whitby and Hull. William Marr was born in Dundee in 1808. As a young man he settled in Hull where he worked as a harpooner on a whaler. He was a strong, tough fella who was 6 ft 3 in tall and full of muscle. He married Rachel Wood, whose parents owned a pub called the Masons Arms. Hunting whales was a dangerous business and vessels were often crushed by ice. Scurvy and frostbite were added dangers and in 1835 William Marr died at sea. In the same year his son Joseph was born. When he died in 1900 he owned fishmongers' shops, ships, fishing smacks and trawlers. Our family ran fleets of trawlers out

of Fleetwood and Hull until the 1980s. Far too often people write about trawlers as if round about 1850 they suddenly began to catch fish in Arctic waters. The whalers knew these waters and when gas and later electricity lessened the demand for whale oil, there was a reservoir of skilled mariners to move to the well-known grounds to fish.

Joseph Marr (1835–1900), who owned several trawlers and fishing smacks.

Chapter 8

The Port of Hull

When I was first asked to write this book my initial reaction was to meet up with my friend John Chandler, who is in his nineties, and he recalled,

If you're looking for memories of the Yorkshire fishing industry, then one bloke you must mention is Edwin Smith. In the 1930s he followed J.B. Priestley every step of the way on what was eventually published as English Journey. *Being Priestley it was a bestseller and Smith's pictures helped to sell it. Born in Bradford, Priestley was also famous for his radio programmes recorded during the war. The man himself noted at the time: 'Hull has an enormous trawling fleet and I was taken to see a new trawler being completed in the old Prince's Dock which is in the centre of the town where you can have trawlers and trams running almost into each other. There were riveters, engineers, carpenters and painters all at work on her so that it was hard to move about.'*

John Boynton Priestley (1894–1984) as usual hit the nail firmly on the head and he pointed out that for every one trawler man at sea there were probably more than 20 men and women working in the support industries. J.B. was taken on a tour of the fish auction area and his description was, as usual, crisp and to the point. He went on,

The Town Docks, Hull, c.1895.

I had a talk with one of the trawler owners who told me among other things that the trawler crews were still a race apart, perhaps the last of the wild men in this famed island of ours, fellows capable of working day and night without food and sleep when the occasion demanded it, and then capable of going on the booze with equal energy and enthusiasm. They were also intensely loyal to the skippers, he told me, and do not give a damn for anybody or anything else.

Another writer who captured the Hull harbour scene graphically was Joan Ingleby, whose Yorkshire travel books, illustrated by Marie Hartley, were best sellers from the 1950s for more than 30 years. A family friend of ours, Rene Donley who was born in Dent, then in Yorkshire, and who knew Joan Ingleby, pointed out to me a portrait of Hull docks at that time,

The fish dock is a scene of pushing, hurrying, shouting men and boys. On the quayside, silhouetted against the water, are groups of filleters clad in white coats, oilskin aprons, leggings and clogs, wielding knives with deft rhythmic strokes. Men roll kits, boys trundle crates. These people live roundabout and are born and bred to work and love the sea. Someone ought to make an industrial ballet based on the unloading, filleting, packing and despatch of fish.

Hull fishermen traditionally tended to focus mainly on catching cod and haddock whilst across the Humber, their fierce rivals, the men of Grimsby, went in search of a wider variety of fish. With the coming of the railway, Hull publicly boasted that fish sold early in the morning would be sizzling in a fryer the next day.

A map of the fishing grounds around the North Sea.

At the peak of its working life, if the Hull supply failed, 75% of the fish and chip shops in Britain would have had to close down!

The landing of fish set off a very strict timetable of activities. The trawlers docked on the evening tide and unloading was in full swing from 2 am. At 7 am the auctions began. This scene looked chaotic but it was in fact well organised. Each buyer's office had lorries or even railway wagons parked up at the rear. On average, upwards of 1,000 tons of fish were landed each day. Once the loaded transport had departed, then the clean-up process began in preparation for the following day. It was obviously vital that standards of hygiene were vigorously maintained as all customers insisted on the best quality, sweet smelling (even if it was fish!) product being delivered to time.

When I visited the Hull docks in the 1980s I was surprised not so much by the sheer size of the area but that it was dwarfed by support and subsidiary enterprises. Nothing was wasted and everything needed was to hand. There was a fishmeal factory where offal and bits of non-marketable fish were deboned, ground up and cooked and turned into meal suitable for animal feed. There were blacksmiths' forges, carpenters' shops, rope works and ice factories. There were enormous buildings used to produce the huge trawl nets which were made in pieces by women called braiders and assembled by men called riggers.

In 2007 I met with Doris Hammond, who told me,

Four generations of my female ancestors worked as braiders. It were a tough job and you could begin your working life in dockside works. When you was married and had kids you could work at home on piece work and this was my mother's job and I learned from her from the time I were ten and I'm 83 now. The merchants delivered rope and you virtually had to knit part of a net which was huge and when working we hung it on the back of the door. Although it were like knitting, the needles were very different. They were nearly a foot long and about one inch across. You had to hold your needle in your right hand and the rough twine was looped inside the needle and a thing called a lug was used and pulled tight in your left hand. A really good braider could keep up to six lasses

Corporation Pier, c.1890.

at work as needle fillers and as I had five sisters we were a family concern. This played merry hell with your hands and if we were in funds we kept them hard by soaking them in methylated spirits but if brass were short we used our own urine.

We liked working on piece work and the net companies brought the twine to our doors and collected the finished bits of nets. Our family were known as good and fast braiders and so we were often give the cod end, which was more complex and tougher because it had to cope with an end bit full of heavy fish. We got paid more for the cod end and were glad to do it. Just before I was married I worked in the riggers' yard. The riggers who assembled these nets had to be both strong and agile as the nets were hundreds of feet long and were made by hanging them from the rafters. There is nowt so corrosive as sea water and the nets were soaked in a tar compound. You could always recognise a rigger by looking at his hands which were black. What the modern day safety at work people would say about our work I dread to think. They would have shut the bloody lot down!

Even now there is to me no more exciting sight than watching a fishing boat setting off to do battle with the sea. Tugs and trawlers manouevre about and here the odd siren sounds and there puffs of smoke billow out from the funnels, even if they are now diesel-powered. This sight can never be witnessed by the close family. There is still an easy-to-understand tradition that if a trawlerman was waved off by a loved one, this was a sure sign that he was not coming back! I spoke at some length with George Ferndale, who has been studying the history of fishing in Britain for half a century,

Fishing families, like most in the 19th century, tended to have huge families. In Hull the girls often became braiders and the lads went to sea. In the early days of the industry each skipper was allowed to take on apprentices and many were employed when they were very young children. The job was much too hard and dangerous for them and whilst many skippers treated them well, some were very badly abused and when he moved ship a skipper took his

A Hull herring drifter, c.1935.

own bound apprentices with him. Nobody shed any tears when the apprentice scheme was abolished and they were replaced by deckie learners. Like the rest of the crew these newcomers signed on for each separate voyage and could abandon the sea at the end of a trip should they wish to.

You might wonder just why major ports did not concentrate on catching herring and mackerel. The reason is that neither keep very well, even if iced, and this meant that they had to be sold fresh, smoked or salted. All that kippers are is smoked herring; mackerel can also be smoked or tinned but this tended to be carried out in the so-called minor ports. Herring are somewhat migratory and the herring boats toured Britain and landed their catch in a succession of ports. The lasses followed the fleet and waited for the boats to dock before gutting the fish and pressing them initially in salt. There was therefore a chain of herring ports down the coast. The enterprise employed its own people and rented its own designated area within each port but only for a limited period. The fleet consisted mainly of small Scottish boats and although you do need to mention them, these fleets were not a permanent part of the Yorkshire fishing industry.

Hull, however, was almost exclusively concerned with deep sea trawling for fish and species which could be kept frozen until the vessel returned to port. Skipper Derek Keetley recalls,

By the time we returned to port we were all knackered and ready for a brief rest but an idle trawler does not make money and the

Bobbers at work unloading fish from the bowels of a Hull trawler.

vessel had to be turned round as fast as possible, but this was not our job. You can divide this turn-around into two phases which can accurately be described as wet and dry.

The north end of the docks was the wet side where the fish was auctioned, filleted and packed and this had to be done in great haste so that the catch reached the distant markets in prime condition. The men and women working in all seaports have their own vocabulary and Hull is no exception. John Chandler remembers this Hull 'speak' very well,

Once I had worked around the docks for a few years I got to know some of the head bobbers who worked for the owners. They met the trawlers as they docked and their job was to oversee the unloading of the fish. Under them were bobbers who organised several teams of four 'below men' who went down into the fish hold; the unloading was a really organised job. When Priestley was writing, on a busy day there were more than 500 bobbers 'bobbing' about. It was the same in the 1950s and 1960s when I was a frequent visitor. The below men carefully loaded the fish into baskets which were winched up to be received by the tipper, who emptied and weighed the fish. This meant the use of a metal pan fixed to the scale. Then came the dooler man. He could work at high speed and he sorted fish into species and arranged them in head to tail order ready for viewing by the merchants. The better the presentation, the higher the price paid and so it was in everybody's interest to do the job properly. The final job was both wet and mucky and the board scrubbers cleared all the surfaces of the trawler of blood, gore, fish and ice.

It has been estimated that for every trawlerman at sea, there were around ten other people employed in support industries. This picture shows the Thornella *laid up for repairs by the Globe Boiler and Ship Repair Company of Hull.*

Once the trawler had been unloaded and cleaned, the vessel had to be tugged away to the dry area where damage caused by the rough seas was assessed and dealt with. Tomas Ericson, a Dane, had Jewish blood in his veins and escaped to England during the Second World War. After being vetted by the authorities, he found work in the shipyards of Hull and he told me,

I had lots of work in the dry area of the docks and I knew men who examined each trawler carefully to estimate the damage. We all had to work quickly as the turn-around time of a trawler had to be fast. Each trawler company had what we called a ship's husband who was the boss man qualified to move the trawler from the wet to the dry area. They were all tough buggers and were mostly old skippers. They had eyes like bloody hawks and soon spotted major and minor repairs which had to be done. They also knew how long each job was likely to take. I was an engine man and it was more than my job was worth not to deal with faults and deal with them quickly.

Derek Keetley took up this story,

During each voyage we were aware of damage and sometimes we were able to predict this happening and entered the problems in the log. This was reported to the ship's husband on landing and woe betide us if we skimped on this report.

There had to be mutual trust between owners and skippers and some men worked for a single trawling company all their lives.

Chapter 9

The Trawler Owners

A large number of trawling companies were formed at Hull but not many more than a dozen withstood the test of time. During the heydays of the 1950s and 1960s there were several companies operating and although they were in competition there was some contact between them. For example, any incompetent skipper operating out of Hull would be blacklisted and no other company would employ him. Either he could accept a lower position in a crew or seek his fortune in the rival ports of Grimsby or Fleetwood. This meant that each trawler fished for itself and was fiercely independent. It was only in the 1970s during and after the Cod Wars, which were a disaster for the British fishing industry, that trawlers worked in packs.

By the mid 1980s and with the industry in terminal decline, one of the only two companies operating was J. Marr and Son. The Marr vessels were typified by their hulls being painted yellow and this led to them being called 'banana boats'. The company flag was red and white with 'JM' also prominent. Joseph Marr (1835–1900) began as a fish merchant who operated a few smacks in late Victorian times. In 1902 the family business transferred to Fleetwood, but in

1934 the decision was made to operate from both the Lancashire port and from Hull. Lionel Marr, is obviously proud of his trawling past. He has a special affection for the trawler *Jacinta* (pronounced 'Jashinta') which he helped to preserve as a floating museum based close to the Freeport village and docks at Fleetwood. This vessel, however, has a great heritage relating to Hull, as Lionel told me,

She was built for us at Wallsend in Northumberland in 1972 and she soon began to break all previous records. In 1975 she landed 188 tons following a trip around the Icelandic fishing grounds. In 1986 it made economic sense to switch the Jacinta *to Hull and she became the top earning trawler in Britain, when the annual value of her catch was £1.3 million. There were great celebrations in Hull when this happened but things got better. In 1991 at a time when the fishing industry was at a very low ebb she broke yet another record when 230 tons of fish were landed and sold for £270,516. In 1994 she was the top earning British trawler again when her yearly catch was £1.94 million. Looking at our records for that year, this was even more impressive because the* Jacinta *spent two months in dry dock having her engines serviced.*

Lionel Marr amongst the trawling memorabilia on board the Jacinta.

There is no doubt that the *Jacinta* was an example of the peak of trawler design and the vessel is part of both Lancashire and Yorkshire's fishing heritage. Before describing the perfection of the design I must now turn my attention to the development of these modern trawlers from their origins as simple fishing smacks brought to Hull from the Brixham area of Devon in the 1840s.

Trawler design was literally driven by the power source. Initially the only motive force was sail, with a total reliance on the wind but as steam power evolved, the trawlers could be increased in size. The problem of space for the fish was solved by having one hold full of coal and another made up of a battery of bunkers. The hold was for the outward journey and when their supply was finished the crew set to work scrubbing the area clean so that it could be used as a fish room. The bunkers then provided coal for the return journey. Coal for generating steam was a great improvement on sail but it was a dirty business for a ship which had to land clean fish. The greatest innovation was the change from coal to diesel. Many trawler owners were slow to abandon coal as both Lancashire and Yorkshire had large numbers of mines and the canny companies around the docks had shares in the coal companies. They were therefore reluctant to use engines powered by expensive diesel in favour of their private supply of cheap coal. The docks of Hull had areas where coal could be poured from tall chutes directly into the holds and bunkers of the vessels. John Chandler recalls this time,

In the 1950s most trawlers were coal-fired and a main feature of the dock area was the pall of smoke which surmounted it. The engineers at that time had to work really hard to shovel coal into the boilers and were covered from head to foot in coal dust. The chief engineer's job was to keep the trawler running in all weather conditions.

My own grandfather was described by my family as a ship's engineer and I had visions of an officer's cap with gold braid on the rim. This was not true as the old lad had a much harder life than that. He began as a sailor, literally using sails, but in the days of steam he was not so much an engineer as a stoker heaving coal into boilers. He must have known how important it was to keep the movement of the ship going. Trawler skipper Derek Keetley told me,

> *As skipper I was God above, but below in a hell hole was the Devil himself in the form of an engineer. If he failed, then nobody brought home fish and we were all not only out of pocket but quite probably out of a job.*

Even the Royal Navy was reluctant to abandon steam power for the much cleaner diesel fuel and so it is no wonder that most trawling companies were slow to react.

I love going through the archives of these old Hull companies if only because their livery must have provided colour and character to the hardworking docklands. Just as today's children can recognise

---

The chief engineer and fireman at work on the steam trawler Northella *in the 1950s.*

the colours of their local football teams, those living around the docks could recognise the liveries of trawling companies. In addition to the yellow 'banana boat' hulls of the Marr vessels, there was one other company which survived until the 1980s. This was the Boyd Line Ltd which only began operating in 1937. Their funnels were painted red, with a central white band, a logo copied directly from the Hull and East Riding Rugby Union jerseys.

There was also a tendency for trawlers to be given similar names. The Marr trawlers, for example, usually had names ending in –*ella*, e.g. *Primella*, *Lancella* and *Thornella*, whilst the Boyd Line went for more evocative names such as *Arctic Invader* or *Arctic Warrior*. Earlier there was the Newingham Steam Trawling Company, established about 1909, whose flag was a prominent red, white and blue; its vessels followed the literary theme and eventually included *Conan Doyle*, *Rudyard Kipling*, *Somerset Maugham* and *C.S. Forester*. The Cargill Steam Trawling Company originated way back in the days of sail and celebrated the empires of the world by naming their steam-powered vessels *British Empire*, *Roman Empire* and *Indian Empire*.

The list of defunct companies is a long one but a final mention has to be made of the West Dock Steam Fishing Company Ltd which was founded in 1922. This date can be confusing, however, because of a name change. The history of this company actually dates back to the 1840s when the Robins family arrived from Ramsgate with their fleet of fishing smacks. Their flag was blue and showed a seagull in flight. Names of steam vessels also provide a liberal slice of Hull's history. Until 1293, Hull was known as Wyke and the West Dock Company added names of nearby villages, so we have *Boynton Wyke*, *Rosedale Wyke* and *Staxton Wyke*.

This aspect of Yorkshire's fishing industry could well be the subject of major research projects and there is plenty of archive material tucked away in the various museums in and around Hull. There is no space here to go into any more detail because I must turn to the subject of trawler design. By far the best way to do this is to talk to the men who crewed the vessels. Old trawler men are usually young in spirit as they recall life aboard a trawler and

It is no wonder that the crew of this steam trawler in 1910 were prepared to take time out for a photograph – they had just hauled a huge catch of hake.

some have memories from the cramped and uncomfortable days of steam through to the comparatively luxury of vessels like the record-breaking *Jacinta*.

The change from sailing smacks to steam trawlers seems to have been an evolution rather than a revolution. From the 1860s onwards there was an increasing use of steam-driven paddle tugs to bring storm-damaged sailing vessels back to their home ports. From what I can gather, it seems that my grandfather worked on tugs such as those mentioned.

Some tug skippers decided to chance their luck and trawl a net and were so successful that there seemed to be a future in replacing sail with steam, even though the vessels were more expensive to build and operate. It did, however, ensure a much greater range over which to fish. The idea took time to be accepted and even then, it was not Hull which led the way but Scarborough. In 1881 this latter port took delivery of the *Pioneer*, which was 94-ft-long but the canny Yorkshiremen hedged their bets by combining the steam engine with a provision of sails just in case. Also in 1881, Earls of Hull built the steam-driven stern trawler *Zodiac*. This, however, was commissioned for the Great Grimsby and North Sea Steam Trawling Company, which obviously plied its trade out of the rival port of Grimsby. The Hull fishermen did not like this and had their own vessels built.

These steam trawlers were able to operate as far out to sea as Iceland and, by 1891, this was a regular route. The early design faults, however, meant that improvements had to be made and by 1905 larger, more seaworthy trawlers were able to penetrate as far as the White Sea. These steam trawlers dominated the industry but just after the Second World War, oil-burning vessels were beginning to replace them. The first of these vessels in Hull, called the *St John*, was built by Cox, Welton and Gemmell Ltd in their Beverley shipyard. Change in trawler design was instigated first by oil burners and then by diesel engines, and from the 1940s to the 1960s trawling from Hull continued to dominate the catches along the Yorkshire coast.

Chapter 10

Trawlers and Trawlermen

The only way that landlubbers like me can appreciate how tough life was for a trawlerman is to talk to as many of these old salts as possible. Even this is not good enough – you need to wander round the bowels of a trawler to really get the atmosphere of the vessel. Here I was lucky, as I was able to go aboard the *Jacinta*, with Lionel Marr. His words summarise the workings of a trawler,

It's difficult to imagine just how hard life was in the old trawlers. I'll take you round the Jacinta *but you should remember that she was at the peak of development and she was without doubt the most successful of all the Hull vessels in terms of profits. We owners loved her to bits. One thing is deceptive and that is how small the trawler looks from a distance, but once inside the interior is vast and no inch of space is wasted. Part of the fish hold has been restored to show its original function and is divided into metal cages called pounds. Here the fish were packed in ice and close by is the fish room, but it is more accurate to call this the factory area. The fish from the nets was pushed down into chutes where men were waiting to gut the catch. This was a real improvement to*

The 'ice pounds' of a trawler.

what went on in the early days when all the gutting was done on deck, often in freezing conditions. You had to gut the fish as soon as possible because it was full of bacteria which would soon cause the fish to rot. In the Jacinta *the guts went down chutes which fed directly into the sea and were eagerly awaited by the seabirds that always followed a vessel as the fish was being processed. One piece of the gut that was not discarded was the liver, which was placed in a huge drum. This produced cod liver oil, which was sold on landing and the money went directly to the crew as a financial perk.*

From the fish factory Lionel took me up to the bridge, which is now gleaming and so well restored that it looks to have come directly from the maker's yard. A latter-day skipper had to be both a first-rate navigator and something of an electronic whiz-kid. Skipper Derek Keetley takes up this theme,

You had to understand the radar and electronic equipment, which was so sophisticated that you could detect not only the navigational hazards but also shoals of fish. By the 1980s you became so skilled that you could even tell from the echoes which species of fish were present. All skippers had long conversations with the old timers who told us how hard life used to be. All of us read quite a lot during trips and I spent some time studying the history of trawlers. What a fascinating story this is.

Even after the nets had been hauled, the trawler crewmen still had plenty of work to do – the fish had to be gutted, sorted and stored.

Derek found me books on the history of trawling from its earliest days in the 1880s. Until the 1890s beam trawling was the only way to catch large quantities of fish but things began to change as sail was replaced by steam power. By the advent of the First World War, steam-powered vessels made up the majority of the fleets.

The Hull firm of Kelshaw Bros and Beeching, founded in 1894, had an impressive fleet which briefly operated out of Fleetwood where they were closer to the fishing grounds and therefore used less coal. By 1897, however, they had returned to Hull. Their flag consisted of a red cockerel on a white flag and the funnels of their

The so-called 'cod end' of the trawling net was subject to such pressure that it was protected by sheets of leather.

vessels were mainly red with a black top. They were either named after birds such as the *Raven*, *Crane* and *Owl* or else ended in *–ic*, e.g. *Oceanic* and *Teutonic*. For some reason which does not seem to be clear, the company suddenly folded in 1936 but this may have had something to do with the Depression.

Lionel Marr has family memories of his own company in this transition period and commented,

> *Steam trawlers caught more fish and at a faster rate but they were more expensive to run because of the fuel and they were also larger, with a bigger crew who had to be fed and paid. There were three brothers operating at that time and the risks taken by Joseph, James and Herbert Marr proved they had excellent judgement.*

Once the long deep-sea trawlers arrived, there had to be a rapidly developing support structure to deal with the increasing number of vessels landing more and more fish. Maud Jessop, now in her nineties and living with her daughter in Brisbane, Australia, remembers Hull in its 'heavenly heyday' as she called it,

The docks to me looked like heaven as they provided us all with work but it was such a noisy spot that it sounded like hell with Old Nick at an anvil all day and most of the night. Ships' chandlers did a roaring trade and so did the riveters who repaired iron plates and the rope makers who delivered supplies to the riggers repairing damaged and/or replacing towing cables. There were blacksmiths, plumbers, tinsmiths, pipefitters, braiders, net-makers and boilermakers. My family, including father, brother and uncles, were all joiners and my husband's family were shipwrights None of us were short of work in the 1950s and 1960s. Most lads that I went to school with had fathers who were seamen in steam trawlers and who told them how much easier life was when steam gave way first to oil and then to diesel, resulting in bigger and more comfortable ships.

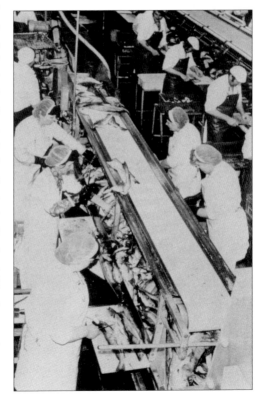

Cod being filleted at the Findus Frozen Food factory in Hull.

Fish for sale at St Andrew's Dock, Hull, c.1935.

Harry Tomlinson told me of one job done on steam trawlers which not many people know about,

> Boilers got sooted up and, in the confined space of a trawler's boiler room, cleaning out the pipes was a real struggle. Young boys or men with small stature were employed to do this job. They discovered that painting the pipes with cement wash meant that they did not block up as quickly.

At the end of the Second World War oil-fired boats began to be built and in 1945 the Marr Company built the *Southella* which traded out of Hull. Although fuel oil was cheap then, Lionel Marr set this change in context:

> The steam trawlers at this time had reached a peak in their development and some of our ships were popular with the crews. First the oil-fired steam trawlers were a wonderful hybrid, but

Fish being landed from the side of the diesel-powered Hull trawler, Falstaff. This was operated by Hellyer Brothers Ltd.

when diesel engines began to operate without the need to boil water it was obvious we had to think about a change. These engines were more powerful and meant the trawlers could be bigger and allow more comfort and safety for our crews. There was also more room for fish.

The first obvious design change was that the once essential tall funnel designed to keep smoke away from the wheelhouse was not necessary. Instead the funnel, which was really an exhaust, was incorporated into the superstructure and gave the trawler a much more streamlined and attractive appearance. These vessels were called sidewinders, simply because the nets were hauled in over the side.

From the late 1960s, however, the diesel-powered stern trawlers meant that the nets could be hauled from the stern and this heralded a radical change in design, as Lionel Marr told me,

The sidewinders had their main superstructure situated amidships and then running aft. When the stern trawlers came on stream it meant that there was a low foredeck and the accommodation was

The sidewinder trawlers were very impressive vessels. The Kingston Wyke was built in Beverley and was 205 ft long.

relocated forward. The net was hauled over the stern and the crew had both more room to move about and much more shelter from the elements. We ordered a number of these vessels, some of which were built by Cook, Welton and Gemmel at their yard in Beverley. It was a great pity because these stern trawlers came too late; by the 1970s the fishing industry was in decline and most were being salvaged as scrap from the early 1990s onwards.

However well designed and constructed a trawler was, the only thing that mattered to all in the fishing industry was the efficiency of the crew, as Derek Keetley told me,

In the crew there was no short cut to promotion because men in charge without experience were a hazard. There was no such thing as influence because you started at the bottom and worked up. Most of us began as young lads and we were called deckie learners. Once you got your sea legs after a few trips you could work on deck. Then you became a deckhand and if you did your job right you were promoted to second deckhand and then third deckhand. After a good number of days or even years at sea, you could be promoted first to bosun and then to a mate. The skipper was in charge of the running of the ship but the mate was in charge of all the work which occurred on deck and in the fish holds beneath. When a mate did his job well the fish arrived in tip-top saleable condition. We all knew that a really good mate found it hard to become a skipper because owners provided him with lots of incentives to stay in this position.

A skilled deckhand was literally worth his weight in gold. Great skill was needed in sorting and packing the fish on shelves, with wooden struts between them to prevent crushing.

Ship's engineers also had their hierarchy but worked independently of the fishing crew. From as long as I can remember, the conversation around the houses of my maternal relatives centred on what it was like to be a fireman shovelling fuel into boilers with a high sea running and threatening to spill hot coals onto your feet. When steam gave way to diesel most of the danger disappeared and the firemen became greasers or third engineers. The chief engineer was the dominant figure and heaven help the poor devil who did not look after his engines, which resulted in a breakdown. A ship standing still cannot make a profit. The best engineers, however, were capable of carrying out repairs at high speed.

In times of Arctic sub-zero temperatures the engineers were able to enjoy more warmth than the trawling crew, but gradually shipowners realised that the more comfortable the crew were, the more efficient they would be. This aspect was underlined by Lionel Marr aboard the *Jacinta*,

> *As you look round this trawler, you have to realise that she was most comfortable for the crew. You should remember, however, that this was not a cruise liner but a working vessel which had to make a profit and not an inch of space was wasted. Compared to the bad old days, the crew of the* Jacinta *and all other trawlers of this period were well catered for in terms of comfort. Even the gutting was not carried out on the open deck but within the drier area of the fish room.*

When Lionel Marr showed me the galley of the *Jacinta* I was reminded of a well-run hotel kitchen, except that the plates and cooking utensils were firmly secured in racks. I spoke to Mick Rodgers, who began his life at sea as a galley boy in the 1950s,

> *It took me a long time to adjust to the hard life at sea when the welfare of the crew was less important than it was later. I remember peeling spuds in a storm, with utensils crashing about all over. I was busy being sick, as well as trying to stop a bucket of potatoes from moving. What saved me was the rest of the crew. One deckhand told me to lie down or throw up while he did my job. I spent more than 30 years as a deckhand but I'll never forget my year in the galley. Fishermen work very hard and they need plenty to eat to keep their energy levels up. In the 1950s there was no refrigeration apart from the natural low temperatures in the Arctic and keeping food fresh was a problem. We used tinned milk, ate lots of fish and the cooks baked fresh bread every day. There was nowt like coming off duty to be greeted by the smell of fresh bread, coffee and the*

'Frozen fear' – ice was a constant danger to the trawler crew.

sound of frying bacon. Our diet when on the fishing grounds was 98% fish but fresh fish can't be beat, can it?

Skipper Harry Chandler made this point very clearly,

It's obvious that a hungry crew can't work properly and so meals were organised to a strict timetable. Breakfast was at 06.30, dinner at 12.30 and tea at 18.00. The work pattern for the crew was a lot more flexible because it depended upon the hauling of the nets and when we were among the fish there was no rest for any of us. Normally the crew worked on an 18-hour-on and a 6-hour-off shift; and you mustn't think that the deckhands didn't do any skilful jobs. Apart from maintaining the gear in good order, the lads learned to steer the boat whilst on watch and they also learned the charts, to help them move up to be coxswains, mates and then to skippers. The last trawlers I was on until I retired in the 1980s were palaces compared to the boats I trained in. The old steam trawlers had very cramped conditions and when a heavy sea was running the waves would wash into the bunks. The new designs which came with the coming of the diesel engines meant that the living quarters were placed in a more sheltered area and were obviously drier but they were also much warmer.

It was good that you only had to battle with one enemy and that was the unforgiving sea. Whatever ship you were in, ice was a constant hazard in an Arctic winter. If ice built up on the rigging, the ship would become top heavy and capsize. At this time all the crew were busy chopping away the ice which was a hard job because just as one block of ice was cleared another formed. You either worked or you drowned and so you worked.

Chapter 11

The Cod and Conflict

Throughout the First and Second World Wars, the trawler men had two tasks. Firstly they had to support the war effort, but they also had to supply fish to a hungry population enduring a strict rationing regime.

By far the greatest threats to a hungry nation dependent upon imports of food were the U-boats and mines. Sweeping the channels free of electronically-primed magnetic mines was a vital job and because trawlers were composed mainly of wood, which did not attract the mines as metal would, they were perfectly designed to act as minesweepers. From 1939, Winston Churchill set up Operation Fish which involved requisitioning a trawler's crew, including the skipper. Each boat was commanded by a young Royal Naval officer but everybody knew who was boss and that was the experienced trawler man.

Joyce Openshaw, who was a director of the Iago Trawling Company based in Fleetwood, told me,

At the beginning of the war our best trawlers were requisitioned for the war effort but we could carry on trawling with our old

Hull trawlers such as the Kingston Amber *did sterling service during the Second World War.*

vessels and we even had to bring some out of retirement. This also happened at Hull and because of the fact that this port was on the north-east coast and was closer to the enemy, many of their old trawlers came to fish out of Fleetwood. A good fish catch, however, was diverted to Hull in order to provide food for this area and because it was linked to the railway network.

The fishing fleets did recoup some of their losses after the war when purpose-built minesweepers were sold off at knock-down prices. They were soon adapted to brave the Arctic weather and bring home vast volumes of fish. The 1950s and 1960s really were a boom time for the fishing industry as Helen Martin related,

I lived with my parents in Hull all through the war. Dad was a shipwright and mum was still braiding nets although she was not as busy as she had hoped. Most people expected that once the war was over, times would be hard but for us life was wonderful. Work

*in the yards was hectic and there was overtime on offer as there was
a never-ending demand for nets. This continued until well into the
1970s but the Cod Wars were a bigger disaster for us than either
of the two world wars.*

This is certainly true and no fisherman in Hull will ever forgive
the British politicians of all parties who did more damage to the
trawling industry than U-boats or mines ever did.

From the 1950s, foreign governments began to extend the
territorial limits of their waters on the pretext – probably without
much foundation – of conserving fish stocks. Many countries were
doing this but the real bone of contention was with Iceland. At
that time there was a strong Communist element in Iceland and
they would have preferred to have a Russian base on the island.
However, they needed the American base to close before this could
happen. With the release of one-time secret papers, it is now possible
to see that it was our own politicians who betrayed the trawling
industry. The Americans wanted to keep their base and therefore
the British government gave in to pressure to allow Iceland to
extend its fishing limits to first 12 miles and then to 200 miles.
As if this was not enough, a further blow was dealt to the British
fishing industry which has also just very recently been brought
to light. Prime Minister Edward Heath was so desperate to get
Britain into the Common Market that he was prepared to accept
any clandestine deal in order for this to happen. As a condition
of entry, Heath secretly agreed to divide up the fishing grounds
around Britain and the North Sea, with the major share going to
German, French and Spanish fleets.

Despite this European sell-out, the focus of attention was still
on Iceland which, with American blessing, planned to extend its
territorial waters despite a ruling against it by the International
Court of Justice. In 1975, in defiance of that court ruling to the
contrary, the Icelanders imposed a 200-mile limit. Many British
trawlers chose to ignore this limit which resulted in what became
known as the Cod Wars. Icelandic gunboats became ever more
aggressive and even cut trawling gear adrift. There were some

A trawler being confronted by an Icelandic gunboat during the Cod Wars.

Royal Navy vessels close by but they did very little to help the fishermen, no doubt because of the Anglo-American agreement not to push the Icelanders into the hands of the Communist Soviets.

It is in this context that the fate of the Hull trawler *Gaul*, without doubt the most controversial incident in the whole history of the fishing industry, needs to be examined, whose loss has not been fully agreed upon even to this day. This 200-ft-long stern trawler registered in Hull as H243 was sunk with all hands on 8th February 1974. She was owned by British United Trawlers Limited and she sank in the Arctic Ocean. The last contact with her was 70 miles off northern Norway.

It is sad to report that many unscrupulous journalists went in search of a good story first and accurate facts came a very poor second. This has caused far too much grief for bereaved families as the controversy has gone on for so long. Were the nets of the *Gaul* caught by a Russian nuclear submarine on a secret Cold War mission? Probably not! Was the *Gaul* kidnapped and the crew taken

The major confrontations during the Cod Wars took place between 1975 and 1976. Here the British frigate, HMS Galatea *is keeping watch on the Icelandic gunboat,* Odinn.

prisoner? Almost certainly no. Was the Gaul carrying secret spying equipment to keep an eye on the Russians? Doubtful. Whatever her fate, the *Gaul* is still posing questions.

Trawlermen who were present in the area are convinced that the *Gaul* was struck by a freak wave at a time when all of her hatches were open and with the crew on deck hauling the nets. I spoke at length with Mick Rodgers who was a deckhand on the *Celt*, which was a sister ship of the *Gaul,*

We set off to fish along with the Gaul *into the Arctic which was always a rough, cold spot. The* Celt *had a rough passage outward and we put into a Norwegian port for minor repairs and so got separated from the* Gaul, *but we knew more or less where she were bound. When the news came through that she were lost with all hands we had a problem because five of our crew had family members on the* Gaul. *These five were flown home and replaced by new lads. We had to keep fishing because if you don't fish you don't get paid. Our skipper was Kenny Madding who was a great chap and he kept us all informed of the progress of the ten Royal*

Navy ships engaged in the search. It may have been the presence of so many Navy vessels in the area that led to the newspaper chaps going overboard in search of a story about the Russians. Most of us thought that these reporters should have been chucked overboard. Our opinion was then, and still is, that the Gaul was hit by a freak wave during a heavy storm and we knew that this was a danger that we all had to face.

Much later, five bodies were recovered and DNA tests have shown that they were men from the *Gaul*. Obviously this gives no indication of how the vessel was sunk but it does at least dispel the rumour that the crew were kidnapped by the Russians. Losing a loved one is bad in any event but not being able to locate the body is much, much worse. Nobody knows this better than Sam Barton, who lost his father at sea,

I was seven years old when the Fleetwood trawler Evelyn Rose went down on New Year's Day 1954. My father was Chief Engineer on board and my mother never recovered. I have spent most of my life searching for the wreck. We found her in 2007 and I'm now trying to bring back the remains of my dad. I know how these Gaul families in Hull feel and the last thing they want is journalists in search of a story opening up old wounds.

There are two other areas of conflict involving trawlers which have seldom, if ever, been properly documented. Firstly there was the Dogger Bank incident, probably more accurately known as the Russian Outrage, which took place on 21st October 1904. The Hull-based Gamecock fleet of 40 trawlers was fishing around the Dogger Bank some 200 miles from Spurn Head and among the vessels were the *Hawk*, *Owl*, *Raven*, *Crane*, *Gull*, *Mino*, *Moulmein*, amongst others. At this time the Russians were at war with Japan and their substantial Baltic Fleet, which consisted of seven battleships, six cruisers and several torpedo boats, was on its way to Port Arthur in the Far East when, early on that fateful morning they made contact with the fishing fleet.

The crew of the Mino *trawler standing beside the damage suffered by the vessel during the Dogger Bank incident of 1904.*

For some unknown reason the Russians mistook this British fishing fleet for Japanese torpedo boats. They turned on their searchlights and opened fire. It was the *Crane* which took the brunt of the onslaught and Skipper George Smith and third hand William Leggett were killed instantly whilst other members of the crew were very badly wounded. It soon became obvious that the *Crane* was sinking and her crew were taken aboard the *Gull* even though the trawler herself was a shattered wreck. The *Mino* and the *Moulmein* sustained superficial damage to their superstructures.

It took some time for the Russian Fleet to realise its error but even then the stricken trawlers were given no help and the Tsar's navy steamed away. When the trawlers returned to Hull, the tight-knit local community was outraged and a relief fund was opened to help the relatives of the dead and those injured. King Edward VII donated 200 guineas and also made contact with the Tsar, as all the European monarchs were at that time closely related. There were official protests to the Russian government who agreed to court martial those officers responsible and also pay £65,000 to the relief fund.

In the final event neither of these things happened, as in May 1905 the Russian fleet met the Japanese and were devastated in the Battle of Tsu-Shima. The only result was that Henry Smirk, the Chief Engineer of the *Gull*, and William Smith who was the mate aboard the *Crane* were each awarded the Albert Medal. There is a

The statue of George Smith, skipper of the Crane *that was sunk by the Russians in 1904, stands on the Boulevard at Hull.*

memorial to the victims of the Russian outrage on the Boulevard at Hull and among the collection of artefacts in the Hull Museum are some items damaged by Russian shells on the *Mino.*

The second area of conflict serves to underline the truth that a succession of British governments have been prepared to make use of the trawler fleets when it suited them but not to support them politically when the need arose. I am sad to have to write this, but fisherfolk have plenty of facts to support their case.

When the Falklands conflict came to a head in 1982, the Admiralty immediately pressed into service some of the best of the trawlers which were still allowed to operate out of British ports. The trawlers were used as minesweepers and support vessels and, as usual, were in the thick of the action. Lionel Marr showed me a dramatic photograph taken in October 1982, at the end of the conflict. It shows five of the family-owned trawlers passing under the Forth Bridge on their way home. Once again, though, the British fishing fleets were ignored and their decline allowed to continue. It is no wonder that trawler men and their families feel bitter as they themselves drift into history.

A postcard that was distributed marking the Russian outrage in 1904.

Chapter 12

Hull

The Decline and Fall of a Proud Fishing Port

My diary dated 3rd August 1993 has one of the saddest entries that I have ever recorded,

> *A visit to Hull Docks close to Draper's Yard. I looked at some still wonderfully efficient trawlers being moved by tugs to be demolished and sold for scrap. Most of these vessels were built in the 1970s and had years of work left in them. Not far away old fisherfolks' houses were being demolished and standing gaunt against the grey skyline; and glistening in the heavy rain were front doorways where once the nets of braiders were hung.*

I was in the company of Doris Jackson, whose parents and grandparents were Hull born and bred,

> *When I look at this bloody carnage I can see my history disappearing before my eyes. They say that all industries decline and fall but it is a*

113

The freezer steam trawler, Junella, *docking at Hull in July 1962.*

bit stupid to devastate an industry which is a food source for all of us. My dad was a trawler man all of his life and he will never forgive the politicians who actually helped to plot the downfall.

This is not just a self-interested worry but is a factual explanation of what happened and why much of the fish we now pay for is caught by foreign trawlers in waters

Fresh and frozen fish being unloaded from the Junella.

pioneered by British seamen. We have only just managed to hang on to our inshore fisheries like those already described in the Whitby, Scarborough, Filey and Bridlington areas.

Dick Gillingham mentioned to me how surprised he was that it took as much skill and care to dismantle a ship as it did to build one. Colin Evans confirmed this,

> *I was pleased to have a job in the 1980s and1990s and one which paid well but at the same time I were sad because I knew that the job would not go on forever. There are only a limited number of trawlers to break up. I were a trained welder so I were used to using a mixture of calor gas and oxygen to provide the heat to cut up trawlers. It was hot work and in the pubs after work I met with other tired chaps who were in the demolition work. They had to be careful at first because there was lots of expensive and quite new items which could be sold on.*

Speaking to a number of former trawler owners, including Lionel Marr, it became clear that all firms had been undergoing hard times and some of the sophisticated radar and radio equipment they used was actually on lease. There was also a ready sale for good lifeboats and brass fittings which were sure of fetching a good price. Some of these items were actually stripped out whilst the vessels were tied up alongside the William Wright dock before being tugged to their final resting place at Draper's Yard. There was a tried and trusted method of breaking up trawlers at Draper's. John Parrington told me,

> *The first job was to tie up the vessel and allow her to settle in the muddy bottom. There was more of a problem with newer vessels because their fuel tanks had to be cleared out. Once you start using cutting equipment you need to keep fuel vapours well away. The fuel was pumped out and the tanks thoroughly washed with seawater from the Humber and only then could the cutters and the cranes be moved in. The rails and the wall area of the ship were cut away and walkways constructed so that the demolition teams*

The end of a proud industry. This picture shows modern stern-freezer trawlers having to be laid up in Albert Dock, Hull, in 1978.

could move about freely. During cutting up, fire could be a hazard. If the timber could be recycled, then this was done but if there was no market for it then there were controlled burns. I know many chaps who made a bit on the side by selling wood to folks who still had open fires. The most difficult job was to try to remove the engine room and some of these diesels had years of life left in them and were very powerful pieces of kit.

By this time the once proud vessel had become a pirated fire-damaged hulk and was removed by tugs to the Hedon Road area, where the final 'bones' of the vessel were cut up and transported to scrap metal merchants in search of a bargain.

It was not just the trawlers and the fishermen's houses, shops and pubs of Hull which disappeared but the once vibrant fish docks were also in the cruel hands of the developers. When the *Arctic Raider* of the Boyd Line with her cherry red and white banded funnel sailed out of St Andrew's dock on 31st October 1975 at 04.00 hours, she was the last trawler to set off for the fishing grounds. She left the dock empty for the first time in 92 years. Three years later the once huge fleet of sidewinder trawlers had disappeared forever and everybody in the port knew that the end was nigh. In 1988 the dock itself was demolished and replaced by characterless fast-food outlets and amusement complexes.

Gone were the days when fish was cheap, as catches were reduced and the price of fuel spiralled. There is no doubt that there was a shortage of fish due to over fishing but the over fishing was predictable and preventable and would never have happened in the old days when fish was farmed rather than exploited. This point was made to me when I interviewed the ornithologist Athol Wallis at his home near Filey,

> I've been a bird watcher mainly concentrating on the Yorkshire coast and its colonies of seabirds. Over more than 40 years I got to know the coastal fishermen and to a lesser extent those who operated in more distant areas. All these men were sea farmers rather than exploiters merely in search of profits. These old-timers understood the biology of the seabed and how the fish they caught fed and maintained the food chain. The activities in the old days did not affect the bird populations at all because they fed on small fish such as sand eels. The new-fangled and much larger foreign trawlers which now have leave to fish our waters do not just use huge nets, often with the illegal small meshes; they also use an electronic device to hoover up all creatures from the sea bed. Not only do they catch marketable fish but they also catch tons of small fry which are converted into animal feed. This has led to a decline in birds such as puffins, razorbills and guillemots which suffer from a shortage of their natural food.

Trawlermen have long memories and have yet another reason to think they have been unfairly treated, and it is impossible to disagree with their logic. Derek Keetley made this point very clearly,

> There were rules imposed which permitted a trawler to land only a designated weight of fish. If they had a particularly heavy net and the quota was exceeded, then any excess had to be dumped at sea. The fish were fresh and excellent to eat but had to be thrown back even though they were dead. What a scandalous bloody waste.

Another death knell for the trawling industry was an extension of the quota system which meant that any vessel was only allowed to put to sea on a fixed number of days. This meant that a trawler was forced to lay idle and, as history has taught us, any idle trawler is a drain on finances and an economic disaster waiting to happen. I have spoken to many trawler men who tell me, off the record, that Spanish trawlers flout these rules but employ British skippers who know the fishing grounds. The skipper is in charge of 'foreign crews' whose wages are much below those which British deckhands need to keep body and soul together.

At this time the Boston Deep-Sea Fisheries and the Marr Company had tried without success to fish in Canadian, South African and Australian waters, but these countries obviously had their own fleets and the markets proved impossible to break into.

Is the Yorkshire fishing industry just a memory? Thankfully the answer is not quite. Sea fish has certainly become a luxury item and over-fishing has meant a proliferation in fish farming but small inshore fleets around the coastal resorts are still working and carrying on a centuries-old tradition.

The purpose of this book has been to record the memories of those who were at the forefront of the fishing industry and can remember the days when it was at its peak. In November 2010 I had conversations with Lionel Marr, David Pearce, who is a much-respected journalist, and Dick Gillingham, whose historical memory of the industry is encyclopaedic. I also met up with Les Hall, an ex-trawler man I first encountered on a hospital ward in 1971. We are both still going strong and Les returned to the sea. Through this formidable quartet I was made aware of the work of Jim Williams, who was the mate aboard a vessel called the *Arctic Corsair,*

She was part of the fishing industry which has seldom been recorded and yet was a vital cog essential to the smooth running of any trawler fleet. The Arctic Corsair *was an ocean-going tug and her role was to locate and tow home any stranded vessel. She was obviously providing a vital service as a trawler was a very expensive vessel and repairs had to be carried out at her home port.*

David Pearce made the point,

> *I think that your book should not just concern itself with the fishermen but you need to cover support industries as well, especially the social life which played a vital role. Most fishermen enjoyed a drink or perhaps two, three or even more. Usually this involved just the men but many wives were tough enough and cute enough to waylay their menfolk and grab some of their wages before they squandered it in pubs and clubs. In one sense Hull differed from all other trawler ports by having a distinct fisher folks' region which was in and around Hessle Road. Here there were several pubs, including the Star and Garter which must have*

St Andrew's Dock in the 1930s prided itself on delivering fresh fish all over Britain. Some 350 vans, loaded with fish, left the dock each day.

been a rough place. It was not known as the Star and Garter but as 'Raynor's'. Raynor was a long-serving landlord who was well capable of keeping unruly customers in order! Raynor's was also famous for having the longest bar in the whole of Hull. We all regret the insensitive demolition and rebuilding which has led to St Andrew's Dock being smothered in bowling alleys, cinemas, fast-food outlets and other modern-day amenities.

Lionel Marr remembers those good old days,

In its heyday the huge dockland complex operated on two sides. One side was the fish landing area and once the catch had been unloaded the vessels were moved to the opposite side where they were repaired, refuelled and made ready for the next sea fishing trip. Things are very different these days. Modern trawlers still have a basic fishing crew, plus a new-fangled group known as the 'packing crew'. These consist largely of untrained and not very well paid youngsters who work in the freezing area and put fish into boxes. This means that the fish landing areas are no longer needed and the catch goes straight into freezer lorries and then off to markets. Some of the new vessels are huge and have crews in excess of 100 although only fifteen or so are involved in the actual catch.

When the fish dock was operating at full swing, there was plenty of work for everybody but not all went smoothly. I interviewed one trawler man who wished to remain anonymous and he told me:

The trawler men were certainly ripped off which led to a series of fishermen's strikes in the 1970s, which lots of our lads agreed with. We felt that the trawler owners did not declare the true weight of the catch and this meant extra money for them. The lumpers also pinched lots of fish which was never weighed. You could see them going home with their oilskins concealing our valuable fish. It was difficult for fishermen to get together because we were almost always at sea and most men spent only one or two days in port. Eventually we did organise strikes but sadly it did neither side any good.

Even off-comers have our sense of history and I found this out when I was in the Royal Air Force on the island of Malta in the late 1950s. I worked with John Galea, who was a sergeant in the Maltese Air Force. After he retired from the air force, he re-kindled his interest in fishing and his family still have fish stalls on Malta. He told me:

The Brits and the Maltese know the sea because we are island people. My grandfather worked in Hull for a while and he was a boxer.

At first I was confused but John went on to explain that his grandfather was a deckhand on the 'boxing fleet'. Even the huge fish market at Billingsgate in London relied on fresh Hull fish and the fishing smacks remained at sea often for a month or two at a time but sent a daily catch packed in boxes to a carrier vessel. This was the fastest sailing vessel available and soon sped on its way to the port of London. In 1865 these fast sailing vessels were replaced by steam trawlers, which were purpose-built at Stockton-on-Tees. The first to go into service were the *Wellesley* and the *Lord Alfred Paget*, and it is not stretching the truth too far to suggest that this dynamic duo were the forerunners of the steam trawlers which have been described in previous chapters. They were so successful – despite competition from the railways – that two more vessels were commissioned: the *Hallet* and the *Frost*, each capable of carrying 3,900 boxes of fish. These boxes were skilfully packed, like sandwiches comprising fish and ice.

The boxing fleet was based at Hull and was controlled by a supremo who was called the Admiral. Despite competition from an improving railway network, it was still operating until the coming of the Second World War. Vessels such as the *Esmeralda*, owned by the Great Northern Fishing Company and which was built in

The 'boxing' fleets collected boxes of fish from conventional fishing vessels and delivered the catch to lucrative markets, including London's Billingsgate. The Esmeralda *was built in 1903 and gave sterling service.*

1903, were regarded as the best of a good crop of vessels. As John said:

This was one hell of a dangerous job. The seamen had to transfer the boxes from a fishing vessel to the boxer even when there was a high sea running and many hardworking chaps were drowned or killed outright as they were crushed against the sides.

Those in search of more memories should holiday along the coast, talk to the fishermen and enjoy eating fresh fish. Following the fish trail is a journey through history and natural history. It is in these places that you will find that the spirit of the fisherfolk of a bygone age is still evident. Those involved were farmers rather than short-term exploiters of the sea. To many people the obvious answer is large-scale commercial fish farming, but is this the solution? Possibly, but a word of warning should be given here. Fish kept in farms need feeding and it has been calculated that for every ton of saleable fish from a farm, three tons of meal has to be expended. This meal is obtained from the sea by scouring the seabed for small species, which restricts the available food for birds and all marine species. This should not be yet another case of out of sight, out of mind!

The linked problems associated with over-fishing and quotas have already been discussed but fisherfolk would want me to stress that it makes no economic sense to throw away perfectly edible, but dead, fish in nets which are so full that quotas are exceeded. It is not as simple as this, because each species has its own quota and the nets are full of a mix of fish. Which trawlerman wants to throw away some fish and keep others? If he and his crew are to make a living, he must continue to seek the most valuable fish and yet discard less lucrative species which are caught in the same haul. There is no doubt that politicians who have never been to sea in their lives need to have a careful look at these draconian laws!

Another solution concerns all of us in Britain who eat and enjoy our fish. We, perhaps more than any other nation, are sticklers for tradition. We still prefer our cod and chips, or perhaps haddock, if we feel posh. In the course of a long working life, I have visited many countries and have enjoyed visits to fish markets – two of my favourite places are on the island of Malta and the huge fish market in Seattle in the USA. A vast array of different fish, few of which are under threat, are eaten and very good they are. We would do well to consider sampling a wider variety of fish.

It may seem strange to end this book with a recipe but it emphasises the vital point that there is no point in catching fish if nobody wants to eat it. As we have toured the Yorkshire coast in search of the memories recorded here, my wife and I have become enamoured with what we have called our Yorkshire fish pie. The recipe will vary according to what fish is available at the quayside but I can do no better than suggest this recipe – not a decline or a fall of the Yorkshire fishing industry but an everlasting memory dating back to at least Viking times and probably long before.

Yorkshire Fish Pie

1½ lbs of potatoes
1 lb of fish pieces (e.g. cod or haddock)
10 ozs of fresh spinach
grated cheese
a large tomato
a knob of butter
2 tablespoons of flour
salt and pepper
lemon juice
1 pint of sour cream or milk

Preheat the oven to 200°C or gas mark 6. Peel and cut the potatoes into chunks; boil and then mash them. Cut the fish into bite-sized pieces and sprinkle with lemon juice. Melt the butter in a pan, add the flour and cook for only a minute. Then stir in the milk and sour cream. Simmer for 5 minutes until the brew thickens and then add the fish. Spoon the mashed potatoes and the cheese into an ovenproof dish and pour on the fish mix. Cover the dish with spinach and finish with sliced tomato. Bake the pie in the oven for 30 minutes and serve piping hot, with garden peas.

* * *

Here then is a mixed diet of history, natural history and a real taste of the sea. This mixed diet has been built into the folk-memory of those who know the Yorkshire coast. Being an island nation we have always had a love of the sea as well as a fear of it – or should that be a healthy respect for it?

Bibliography

Alison Capt. I. E. *Fishing in Britain* (London 1956)

Creed, R. *Turning the Tide* (Backdoor Press, Hull)

Dykes, Jack *Yorkshire's Whaling Days* (Dalesman 1980)

Freethy, Ron and Marlene *Discovering Coastal Yorkshire* (John Donald 1992)

Freethy, Ron *Memories of the Lancashire Fishing Industry* (Countryside Books 2009)

Freethy, Ron *Yorkshire – The Secret War* (Countryside Books 2010)

Gill, Alec *Hessel Road* (Hutton Books 1987)

Gill, Alec *Lost Trawlers of Hull 1835–1987* (Hutton Books 1989)

Gill, Alec *Good Old Hessle Road* (Hutton Press 1991)

Godfrey, Arthur *Yorkshire Fishing Fleets* (Dalesman 1974)

Nicklin, J. *Loss of the Motor Trawler Gaul* (Hutton Press)

Pearson, Gordon *Hull and East Coast Fishing* (Pearson 1976)

Perks, Sir Basil *Tralings of a Lifetime* (*Cumberland and Westmorland Herald*)

Perrot, Roy *Discovering Deep Sea Fishing* (London 1958)

Robinson, R. *The History of the Yorkshire Coast Fishing Industry* (Hull University Press 1987)

Thompson, Michael *Hull's Side-Fishing Trawling Fleet 1946–1986* (Hutton Press 1987)

Thompson, Michael *Hull and Grimsby's Stern Trawling Fleet 1961–1986* (Hutton Press 1988)

Places to Visit

Whitby Museum, Pannet Park, Whitby YO21 1RE.
Tel. 01947 602908

Sea Life Scarborough, Scalby Mills, Scarborough YO12 6RP.
Tel.01723 373414

The Town Docks Museum, Queen Victoria Square, Hull HU1 3DX.
Tel. 01482 222737

Filey Museum, 8–10 Queen Street, Filey YO14 9HB.
Tel. 01723 515013

Index